Foreword by Mary Robinson

# Towards a Culture of
# Human Rights in Ireland

IVANA BACIK

and

STEPHEN LIVINGSTONE

Cork University Press

in association with

The Centre for Cross Border Studies, Armagh

First published in 2001 by
Cork University Press
University College
Cork
Ireland

**British Library Cataloguing in Publication Data**
A CIP catalogue record for this book is available from
the British Library

ISBN 1  85918  313 1

Typeset by Tower Books, Ballincollig, Co. Cork
Printed by Colour Books Ltd, Baldoyle, Dublin

# Contents

# Foreword

MARY ROBINSON

*United Nations High Commissioner for Human Rights*

An encouraging aspect of the search for lasting peace in Ireland is the recognition that human rights have a central role to play. My observation of societies in conflict or emerging from conflict situations leads me to believe that tolerance and co-existence will only take root if grounded in respect for the human rights of all. I am also convinced that strengthening national capacity is one of the most effective ways to promote and protect human rights. I was glad to see the importance of this approach being given tangible effect through the human rights dimension of the Good Friday Agreement and the decision to set up Human Rights Commissions North and South.

The international community is watching the peace process in Ireland with interest and hope. There is a strong desire to see an end to a situation where so many have lost their lives and so much suffering has been caused. There is considerable interest in the emphasis being placed on the human rights dimension and in the two Human Rights Commissions. If they prove their effectiveness they could be models for national commissions in Europe and elsewhere. The incorporation of the European Convention on Human Rights into domestic legislation North and South is another significant and welcome development.

I commend the Centre for Cross-Border Studies for its series of essays on aspects of the relationship between the two Irish jurisdictions, and for focusing on human rights. Although the island we share is small, there are many misconceptions and gaps of knowledge between people living in the North and the South. These essays will perform a useful service in leading to better mutual understanding and co-operation.

# A Human Rights Culture for Ireland?

IVANA BACIK

## Introduction

Can a new human rights culture take root in the Republic of Ireland in the wake of the Good Friday Agreement? If ever such a development seemed likely, that time is now, with the forthcoming incorporation of the European Convention on Human Rights and Fundamental Freedoms (ECHR) into domestic law, and ongoing discussion at European Union level about the adoption of an EU Charter of Rights. At this time incorporation of the ECHR is the more imminent development. In the course of this essay, it is sought to examine the likely effect of incorporation, in the context of existing human rights protection through the Constitution, and experience of the interpretation of constitutional guarantees in Ireland.

The incorporation of the Convention will lead to the creation of a new legal framework for the protection of certain rights, but this alone will not necessarily lead to the development of a human rights 'culture'. More awareness of human rights concepts, and indeed an increase in litigation, may ensue as a result of incorporation. However, a new culture is unlikely to be generated, because although the protection guaranteed to some individual rights will be strengthened by incorporation of the ECHR, the Constitution already protects a very similar set of rights to those guaranteed in the Convention.

Both documents offer protection to a selection of individual, rather than collective, rights; to what are called civil and political rather than economic and social rights. For the development of a genuine human rights culture, it is argued that a fundamental re-evaluation of the conception of human rights is required. The language of rights, as we know it, is just not sufficiently inclusive to enable the creation of a new rights culture capable of having a real effect upon people's lives.

## Concepts of Human Rights

The widely accepted view of human rights is that they are universal, derived from natural law, inherent in people by virtue of their humanity, their moral and rational nature and their capacity to reason. It is posited that there exists a basic core of rights, including the right to life; to liberty; to vote; to freedom from torture; to freedom of expression, thought and conscience.

A problem with this view of human rights, however, arises from their perceived source. Rights are normally spelt out in positive law, expressed through a constitution or bill of rights. But if they are really derived from natural law, inherent in humanity, then it is impossible to define them concisely in a written instrument. A distinction is thus sometimes drawn between 'human rights' and 'civil liberties'. The latter are seen as being positivistic and political in nature; rights which the state has contracted with its citizens, such as the right to vote, or the right to a fair hearing if accused of a criminal offence. The former set of rights, by contrast, constitutes a collection of rights with undefined parameters, not contained in any document but capable of being plucked from the air.

There is another problem with the definition of rights. It is simply not true that there exists a universally accepted body of human rights.

In fact, states differ over which rights they see as worthy of protection. A 'cold war' split exists within international human rights instruments: between first-generation 'civil and political rights', and second-generation 'economic and social rights'. This somewhat artificial binary divide underlies international rights instruments. First-generation rights are guaranteed in one UN International Covenant, second-generation rights in another. Similarly, in a Council of Europe context, the ECHR protects civil and political rights, while the European Social Charter protects economic and social rights.

Although there is some overlap in the two concepts of rights, they are identified with different political and economic ideologies. Civil and political rights, such as the right to free speech, typically guarantee 'private' individuals some degree of protection against the abuses of 'public' state power, but, at least in theory they do not impose any material obligations upon the state, nor do they relate directly to the functioning of the economy. They are valued most highly by those who espouse a market ideology. According to a marxist or socialist perspective, by contrast, economic and social rights are given priority. The right to housing, for example, may be elevated above the right to free speech, and the right to protection against poverty above the right to protection against other abuses of state power. Economic rights are typically not afforded constitutional protection in liberal-democracies, because their effect might be to undermine the existing economic system.

Marxist and feminist writings have developed influential critiques of rights, based on the argument that rights discourse can divert attention away from political reform and into legal disputes, with consequent reliance upon a largely male judiciary drawn from a homogenous privileged background. Moreover, rights may operate to reinforce privilege, since those in positions of power have more effective access to legal forums, and are more likely to meet a sympathetic response when they get there. Entrenched rights have thus tended to operate in the interests of the powerful, not the powerless.

Although these critiques show strong antipathy towards the concept of rights, this is precisely because they focus upon the rights guaranteed in capitalist democracies, the inherently individualistic and competitive civil and political rights. The real experiences of disempowered groups do not easily translate into this type of rights rhetoric, which fails to recognise existing structural inequalities. However, more current thinking among the feminist movement and those on the left, while accepting these limitations, recognises the rhetorical power of rights discourse, and the symbolic importance of the conferring of rights on those who have been historically disempowered.

Indeed, whilst the entrenchment of rights does not necessarily confer any concrete entitlement, and whilst it may in practice lead to their use by the powerful at the expense of the powerless, claims of rights do have powerful rhetorical force. The legal-political context is so firmly defined in terms of rights, that any successful intervention must inevitably be couched in the same terms. Posing political demands in terms of rights makes those demands more easily understood, since rights language is an accessible linguistic currency. Also, because the notion of rights is generally associated with principles of democracy and freedom, the claim to rights is always loaded in favour of the claimant.

Strategically, there are thus very strong arguments for the adoption of rights instruments, even for those critical of the concept of rights. Rights language has a motivational power; it can be adopted and used as a tool by those who recognise and acknowledge its limitations. The prevailing conception of rights as exclusively civil-political can be challenged, so that greater emphasis is given to the social and economic guarantees which have more potential for real change. Although the entrenchment of economic rights would not actually guarantee economic equality, it would at least enable acknowledgement of the extent of poverty and inequality, and provide those on the political left with some scope to address problems of economic inequality within present constitutional structures.

Some recognition of the need for change in rights language is apparent in the content of the draft EU Charter of Rights which, unlike the ECHR or the Irish Constitution, includes guarantees of rights to health care and to social security. It remains to be seen whether these provisions survive in the final version of this document, or indeed if the final document ever becomes binding in the national legal orders of the EU member states. The overhaul of the European Social Charter in 1996, similarly, marked recognition of the need for strengthened commitment to economic and social rights at Council of Europe level. The revision of the Charter enabled the inclusion of new rights, such as the right to adequate housing and the right of protection against poverty. However, the Council of Europe's Charter does not have the same status in member states as the European Convention on Human Rights.

The need for change has also influenced an emerging new discourse about rights, based on what are sometimes called third-generation or group rights, such as the right of the community to an environment free of pollution, or the rights of particular groups to self-determination. These group rights have formed an ideological basis for the campaigns of ecological activists, and more recently for the dynamic international movement against global neo-liberalist economics. This movement, manifesting itself in demonstrations in Seattle in 1999 and Prague in 2000, seeks to undermine the international neo-liberal capitalist consensus, represented by the International Monetary Fund (IMF) and the World Bank, and has challenged the hegemony of these powerful financial institutions.

One of the key ideologists of the new movement, Naomi Klein (2000), has written of a new concept of rights, emerging from the largely underground system of internet-generated information, protest and planning, a system coursing with ideas crossing many national borders. The new rights talk is all about anti-corporatism, from the Zapatistas of Mexico to students in Toronto to anarchists in Seattle and Prague. And yet this new movement, with its developed analysis of the workings of the global economy, is part of a much older struggle; it can be seen as the heir to centuries-old campaigns against feudal landlords, military dictators and multinational corporations.

The campaigns of the anti-corporatists are easily dismissed because their targets sometimes seem absurd; they boycott Nike products, refuse to eat at McDonalds, sabotage Microsoft products. Yet these brandnames are merely metaphors for a global economic system which the anti-corporatists and their allies in the NGO community worldwide condemn as unjust and unsustainable. Their movement is breathing new life into rights language, investing it with an energy to replace that which had dissipated over the years as the existence of countless international human rights instruments had patently failed to tackle global injustices. Through the NGO community at an international level, rights discourse is being invested with new meaning.

Because of this ongoing re-evaluation, documents such as the European Convention, while based on a traditional civil-political model of rights, retain the potential to allow the perspectives of disadvantaged persons to enter the law. Incorporation of the Convention could heighten awareness of the conflicts within society, and might have the potential to generate debate about rights concepts and to politicise disempowered groups, thereby helping to bring about social change. In this sense at least, incorporation of the Convention must be welcomed, even by those suspicious of the concept of rights it embodies.

## A Human Rights culture in Europe – the experience of the ECHR

The Convention provides for a range of civil and political rights which signatory states, members of the Council of Europe, undertake to secure to individuals within their jurisdiction. Among other provisions, it guarantees the right to life (Article 2), to freedom from torture (Article 3), to liberty (Article 5), to fair trial (Article 6), protection of privacy and family life (Article 8), freedom of expression, thought and religion (Article 9), and against discrimination (Article 14). Since its adoption in 1950, it has grown in size through the addition of eleven Protocols.

Economic and social rights are not generally given recognition in the Convention. Nor are the protected civil and political rights framed in a particularly broad way, so that the Convention has been described as essentially minimalist in character. For example, Article 14 deals with discrimination, but only by reference to individual rights, not community, cultural, ethnic or language rights. Moreover, the power of states to derogate from Convention provisions in 'time of emergency', provided for in Article 15, also weakens the protection of the rights guaranteed in the document.

Despite these weaknesses, some commentators argue that the Convention has effectively established a European culture of human rights, in that it empowers individual citizens of member states by giving them the right to apply to the European Court of Human Rights in Strasbourg, once domestic remedies have been exhausted. Because of the workload of the Court, cases take years to come to hearing, but individuals can ultimately receive remedies from the Court for breaches of their rights.

In another way, too, the ECHR has had an impact in generating a human rights culture in Europe. Its influence on the European Union has been increasing in recent years, with the European Court of Justice giving growing emphasis to Strasbourg jurisprudence. When an EU Charter of Rights is adopted, it will derive inspiration from the Convention. Also, the Convention has now been incorporated into the domestic law of almost all member states, with the result that individuals can rely upon Convention rights before their national courts, although with differing effect depending on the mode of incorporation in each state.

## Models of incorporation of the ECHR

There is no set pattern to the impact of the Convention in the different member states, since each connects with the Convention in a way particular to its own legal and political context. Under the recently enacted UK Human Rights Act, for example, judges have the power to award remedies where actions of public authorities are incompatible with the Convention. In relation to legislation, however, judges only have the power to interpret it in accordance with Convention rights, not to strike it down for incompatibility.

This is known as the 'interpretation model' of incorporation. It requires judges to read legislation in accordance with the Convention, even if this means reading new words into the text. Judges thus have to be inventive in their interpretation of statutes, and this can lead to an artificial and sometimes distorted construction of different words and phrases. Where such construction is simply not possible, the courts may issue 'declarations of incompatibility' in respect of legislation found to be in breach of Convention rights. The declaration of incompatibility has no effect on the validity of legislation, although there is a fast-track mechanism to enable Ministers to amend legislation declared incompatible. Indeed, it is envisaged by many that legislation will be amended relatively quickly in this way to avoid political embarrassment. The interpretation approach may in time thus develop into a more advanced system of judicial review.

The political reality in Britain, even now, is that the power of judges as against that of legislators is vastly increased by the Act. This projected transfer of power to the judiciary is a matter of concern to many lawyers in Britain, a jurisdiction without a written constitution, in which the supremacy of Parliament remains a fundamental constitutional principle. It may take some time for the new constitutional order to become accepted. The experience in Scotland, where ECHR rights have been enforceable through the domestic courts since May 1999, is that the vast majority of Convention-based claims have been unsuccessful to date.

## The Irish model of incorporation

Under the terms of the Good Friday Agreement, the British Government committed itself to the establishment of a Northern Ireland Human Rights Commission. This body was set up in 1999, with duties which include making recommendations to government, promoting awareness of human rights, bringing court proceedings, or providing assistance to individuals in doing so. At the same time, the Irish Government agreed to take comparable steps to introduce measures to strengthen the constitutional protection of human rights, with the aim of ensuring a level of protection of human rights at least equivalent to that which will pertain in Northern Ireland.

In particular, the Government agreed to establish a Human Rights Commission with an equivalent mandate to that of the Northern Ireland body. It was envisaged that a Joint Committee of Representatives on Human Rights would then be set up, with the aim of promoting a Charter of Human Rights for the whole island. But the establishment of this framework was significantly delayed by the failure of the Irish Government to set up a Commission until well over a year after the establishment of the Northern Ireland HRC. Apart from the delay, controversy over the appointments to the Commission erupted due to political intervention in the final stages of the selection process. This controversy was only resolved by the appointment of additional members to the Commission. Such unfortunate developments might well cause one to call into question the genuine commitment of the Irish Government to the establishment of an effective human rights framework for the whole island.

The unjustifiable delay in incorporating the ECHR into Irish law also raises questions about government commitment to human rights. Ireland was one of the ten founding member states of the Council of Europe in 1949, was among the first countries to ratify the Convention and was the first member state to allow individual petitions to the Strasbourg Court in 1953. Yet Ireland is now the only member state not to have yet incorporated the Convention into domestic law. Now that the Convention is in force in Northern Ireland through the Human Rights Act, the need to incorporate the Convention has become urgent, given the commitment to ensuring 'equivalent protection' for human rights.

Clearly, the incorporation of the Convention into domestic law could never mark the same fundamental change in legal culture in Ireland that it has done in Britain and Northern Ireland, given the prior existence of an Irish bill of rights. Even if incorporation has little practical impact in Ireland, however, it will have a powerful symbolic effect. As Hogan (1999) writes, the Convention 'provides a politically neutral template for sensitive cross-border dealings which the [Constitution] could never hope to attain'.

The prior existence of the constitutional rights provisions, and concerns about potential conflict between these and Convention rights, have been used to explain our failure to incorporate the Convention before now. There has generally been a lack of debate in Ireland about incorporation at any level, apart from the consideration given to this issue by the Constitution Review Group in their 1996 report. The Group considered that the only way to incorporate the Convention so that it would be superior to legislation or indeed to the Constitution itself would be by way of constitutional amendment, and that such an amendment could take two forms.

First, it could provide for the replacement of constitutional rights by Convention rights, but this would lead to a diminution of some rights, and would mean the abandonment of sixty years of well-established case law developed by our superior courts' use of existing judicial review powers. The Constitution could alternatively be amended through a single provision based on the Swedish model, providing that no law could be enacted contrary to the Convention. But this approach could lead to uncertainty as to which right prevailed in any conflict.

Another approach to incorporation, not considered by the Review Group, would be based upon the UK 'interpretative' model, and would not require constitutional amendment. Such a model would oblige the judiciary to read legislation so that it complies with Convention rights, and give them power to issue something like a declaration of incompatibility where this is not possible. Since our judges have already got extensive judicial review powers under the Constitution, civil libertarians have expressed concern that the interpretation model would be too minimalist an approach, and unlikely to lead to effective enforcement of Convention rights, since the existing constitutional bill of rights would remain superior. In effect, this method of 'sub-constitutional' incorporation would simply allow judges to refer to Convention rights, but would not oblige them to observe those rights.

It is foreseeable that, even with such a minimalist model in place, judges might refer more frequently to the Convention, so that an increased harmonisation of Convention rights and constitutional rights might result. But it is more likely that sub-constitutional incorporation would have no effect on domestic law in practice, since individuals would still have to take cases to Strasbourg in order to ensure enforcement of Convention rights.

## Impact of the ECHR upon Irish law

Despite the fact that its obligations can already be enforced by Irish citizens through the Strasbourg machinery, the Convention has had limited influence on our domestic law. There have been few cases in which a defeat for Ireland before the Strasbourg Court has provoked a change in domestic law in order to comply with Convention requirements. Individual applications against Ireland to Strasbourg reveal a range of complaints, against conditions of detention, censorship matters and the refusal of leave to appeal against conviction, for example, but the Court has ultimately decided against Ireland in a total of eight individual applications. In a seventh application, that of *Lawless*, Ireland derogated from the terms of the Convention under Article 15 and settlements were reached before hearing in several other cases.

The fact that there have been few judgments decided against Ireland may be a reflection of the overlap between domestic rights provisions and those guaranteed in the ECHR, as well as of the active development of Irish jurisprudence on the rights provisions of the Constitution. A practical reason can also be identified: the time and cost involved in taking cases to Strasbourg may put off many potential applicants. Moreover, other findings against Ireland might well have been made in those cases in which settlements were reached. Notwithstanding these general factors, Ireland has generated relatively few individual complaints, and the majority of those cases decided against Ireland have involved family or sexual themes.

The application of *Airey* against Ireland, for example, raised among other issues the question of protection for family rights. The applicant had been unable to access the Irish courts in order to obtain a decree of judicial separation from her husband, because she lacked the financial means to meet the legal costs involved. The Strasbourg Court held that she had been denied access to the courts in breach of her right to a fair trial under Article 6 (1), but she was also held to be the victim of a breach of Article 8, which guarantees respect for privacy and family life.

The next application in which a claim against Ireland was upheld, that of *Johnston*, decided in 1986, also involved family law matters. The applicants, an unmarried couple and their daughter, had been living together for years, but because of the constitutional ban on divorce the couple could not marry since the father had been married already. They only had limited success before the Court, which rejected their argument that the ban on divorce was in breach of their Convention rights. However, it upheld their daughter's claim under Article 8, in that she did not have the same legal status as the child of a married couple.

Article 8 was also successfully relied upon in the application of *Norris*, who challenged the Irish law criminalising male homosexual activity. The Court upheld his claim that the legislation constituted an interference with his right to respect for his private life. As a result of this decision, legislation decriminalising male homosexual activity was introduced, although not for another five years after the judgment. Since *Norris*, decisions have been made against Ireland in three other cases. In a 1992 decision in the *Pine Valley* case, the applicants, holders of outline planning permission, were found to have been discriminated against in terms of their property rights, since they had been treated differently from other holders of outline planning permission.

In the *Open Door Counselling* case, decided a year later, the Court upheld a claim by providers of pregnancy counselling services that the constitutional ban on the provision of information on abortion amounted to a denial of their right to freedom of expression under Article 10 of the Convention. More recently, in *Keegan*, the denial of rights to a non-marital father in Irish law was found to contravene Article 8 of the Convention, since the Court held that the family protected by Article 8 is not confined to relationships based upon marriage.

Finally, and most recently, the Court found against Ireland in two applications decided on the same day, 21 December 2000. In the first, that of *Heaney and McGuinness*, both applicants had ben convicted under section 52 of the Offences Against the State Act, 1939, which provides that a person who fails to give an account of his or her movements or to provide other specified information when so requested by a garda shall be guilty of an offence. Although section 52 had been upheld as constitutional by the Irish Supreme Court, the European Court found that it imposed a 'degree of compulsion' upon both applicants which, in effect, 'destroyed the very essence' of their right to remain silent. In the second application, that of *Paul Quinn*, which also related to the use of section 52, the Court made a finding against Ireland in identical terms.

Some significant settlements have been reached by the Irish Government before claims reached hearing. For example, in 1996 a claim against the state arising out of the applicant's involuntary detention in a psychiatric institution resulted in a settlement for substantial damages. In another case, involving the issue of succession rights for non-marital children, a payment in settlement of £10,000 was made to the applicant before the hearing. At the time the settlement was reached, the Status of Children Act, 1987, which abolished the status of illegitimacy, had already been introduced. In December 2000, an undisclosed sum was paid by the Government by way of settlement to Sean Croke, who had also challenged his involuntary detention in a psychiatric institution under the Mental Treatment Act, 1945. This settlement forestalled the likely outcome of a ruling by the Court that the Irish legislation is in breach of the Convention. Cases now pending before the Court from Ireland include applications on the length of ongoing civil proceedings and a case arising out of the failure by the state to provide suitable accommodation to minors with special needs.

Apart from the cases specifically involving Ireland, the case law of the Strasbourg Court has been used more generally as persuasive authority by judges in several cases before the Irish domestic courts. However, O'Connell (2000) identifies a pattern whereby those High Court judges who use the Convention to bolster their arguments on

Irish law tend to have their judgments upheld by the Supreme Court on grounds deriving from national law instead. He argues that a 'hibernocentric' approach to international instruments is evident at this level. One might wonder, therefore, whether an interpretation model of incorporation would encourage judges to be more enthusiastic in their use of the Convention. Since such a model would not oblige them to enforce the Convention, it might mean no change at all in rights protection.

## Impact of future incorporation of the Convention

Despite these misgivings there are areas where the Convention clearly offers a higher level of rights protection. It certainly provides greater protection for privacy and family rights under Article 8, with a broader interpretation of the protected 'family' than is presently provided under our Constitution. The protection of freedom of expression represents another area of divergence, since this right is framed more extensively in Article 10 of the Convention than in the Irish equivalent, Article 40.6.1.(i). When hearing cases under this Article, the Strasbourg Court has consistently emphasised the need to protect the right to free speech from attack, holding for example in *Tolstoy*'s case that libel awards must be proportionate with a balance between the competing rights of reputation and free speech. Judgments such as this could have a real impact on Irish libel law if they were to become binding on domestic courts.

Incorporation of the Convention could also affect Irish asylum and immigration law. The Convention expressly offers protection against torture (Article 3) and unlawful killing (Article 2), and it is well established that a contracting party to the Convention is responsible under the Convention for expelling an individual to another country where he or she runs the risk of being tortured or killed. This protection is more broadly framed than the rather limited grounds on which persons may claim refugee status under the Geneva Convention, which forms the basis for the Irish Refugee Act of 1996.

Thus, potential differences between the Refugee Act and the ECHR requirements may be identified. In particular, the lack of an oral hearing under the 'manifestly unfounded' procedure provided for by the 1996 Act could be in breach of Article 13 of the Convention, which guarantees the right to an effective remedy. This is of particular significance given the extraordinarily high percentage of claims that are found to be 'manifestly unfounded' at the first stage of hearing under the 1996 Act. Protocol 4 of the Convention, which Ireland has ratified and which should thus be part of the incorporation process, relates to freedom of movement and expulsion of aliens. It may well have implications for the policy of involuntary dispersal of asylum-seekers around the country.

## Impact of incorporation on the Irish criminal justice system

In the context of criminal justice, there is also clear divergence between the rights protected under the two systems, so that future incorporation of the Convention at a more than minimalist level might again have significant effect in this area, particularly for the rights of suspects in police detention. In relation to the right to legal representation, for example, the Supreme Court held in *Lavery*'s case that while an accused held in garda custody has the right of access to a solicitor before being interviewed by the police, there is no right to have a solicitor present during the interview itself.

By contrast, the Strasbourg Court in June 2000 held in *Averill v. UK* that the denial of access to a solicitor for the first 24 hours of the applicant's detention amounted to a breach of his right to legal representation under Article 6. The same day, the Court found a breach of Article 6 also to have occurred in the *Magee* case, where the applicant was denied access to a solicitor for 48 hours. In coming to its decision in *Magee*, the Court noted the highly critical findings of a European Committee for the Prevention of Torture into conditions at the RVC Castlereagh Holding Centre in Belfast, where the applicant had been held. The Court ruled that these conditions made more compelling the need of the applicant to see a solicitor upon being detained there, an approach which might usefully be adopted in Ireland, since the European Committee was also critical of detention conditions in garda stations.

These decisions, although they do not go so far as to guarantee the right to have a solicitor present throughout one's period of detention, appear to offer potential for a stronger right to legal representation than has been offered through the *Lavery* decision, for example.

In relation to the right to silence, the Irish courts have in the past almost invariably upheld statutory provisions restricting that right, but since the decisions of the European Court in *Heaney and McGuinness* and *Quinn*, it is clear that the Convention offers stronger protection against legislative encroachment on that right than does the Constitution. Although the right to silence is not specifically expressed in the

Convention, in *Murray v. UK* the Court affirmed in 1996 that: 'the right to remain silent under police questioning and the privilege against self-incrimination are generally recognised international standards which lie at the heart of the notion of a fair procedure under Article 6.' The Court ruled, however, that adverse inferences could be drawn from silence if specific safeguards exist, and that no breach had occurred in the particular case.

Several months later, in *Saunders v. UK*, the applicant, convicted of theft and false accounting arising out of the Guinness affair, succeeded in establishing a breach of Article 6 following the use in criminal proceedings of self-incriminating evidence given under duress to Department of Trade and Industry inspectors. The Court found that the public interest could not be invoked to justify the use as evidence of answers compulsorily obtained in non-judicial investigations. Saunders' three co-accused were also successful on the same grounds in challenges to the fairness of their trial, following a judgment of the European Court given in October 2000. The cases of *Murray* and *Saunders*, among others, were cited by the Strasbourg Court in the judgments in *Heaney and McGuinness* and *Quinn*.

These judgments indicate that incorporation of the Convention is likely to affect other Irish legislation providing for curtailment of the right to silence. Under the Criminal Justice (Drug Trafficking) Act, 1996, for instance, inferences may be drawn from the failure of a person charged with a drug trafficking offence to mention, when questioned by gardai, a fact which is later relied upon by the defence at the trial. The Offences Against the State (Amendment) Act, 1998, enacted in the wake of the Omagh bombing, contains a similar provision for curtailment of the right to silence in respect of offences under that Act. Moreover, the Minister for Justice has announced further measures designed to limit the right to silence more generally, by allowing inferences to be drawn from failure to answer questions in relation to any offence punishable by ten or more years' imprisonment.

This proposed restriction on the right to silence would place great pressure on suspects to make statements while in custody, and those particularly vulnerable to threats or inducements would be most likely to succumb to such pressure. The likelihood of false confessions will increase, as indeed will the potential for abuse of power by the gardai. Issues have been raised in the past about the way in which confessions are extracted from suspects in custody; the Special Criminal Court recently expressed grave concerns about garda questioning methods used in the *Ward* case.

The potential for abuse would only be heightened by the introduction of greater garda powers over the suspect, particularly given the absence of adequate safeguards for the accused during police detention. The lack of regulation evident here is in marked contrast to the position in England, where persons detained have the right not only to have their interviews recorded, but also to have their solicitors present during their interrogation. Such measures are essential in order to protect against potential police abuses, and their absence may generate future litigation under the Convention.

Once incorporated into Irish law, the Convention may also have an impact on areas of criminal justice other than the rights of those detained. For example, the legislation on asset forfeiture, whereby assets proven on a civil standard of proof to represent the proceeds of crime may be seized and confiscated by the Criminal Assets Bureau, may well come under scrutiny. The constitutionality of the Proceeds of Crime Act, 1996 has been upheld in a number of decisions by our superior courts, but its legality under the Convention may be at issue following the Strasbourg Court's decision in *Welch v. UK*. Here, a confiscation order imposed upon the applicant subsequent to his conviction for drug trafficking offences was successfully challenged on the basis that it amounted to the application of a retrospective criminal penalty under Article 7 of the Convention. The rights of prisoners may also be strengthened by the incorporation of the Convention, judging by some of the Strasbourg Court case law in which the stopping of prisoners' correspondence, for example, has been held to be in breach of Article 8 privacy rights.

In some aspects of criminal justice, however, the Convention offers weaker protection for the accused than the Irish Constitution. The right to jury trial, for example, is expressly guaranteed in the Constitution. Moreover Article 5 of the Convention, which guarantees the right to liberty, allows for preventive detention, whereas the equivalent constitutional provision was robustly interpreted by the Irish Supreme Court to rule out detention in order to prevent a person from committing an offence. This position was altered by the Bail Referendum in 1996, so that the courts can now detain in custody a person accused of a 'serious offence' (that is, punishable by five years or more imprisonment), where they consider it necessary to prevent the commission of a serious offence by that person while on bail. Even now, however, protection of liberty in the Constitution is still framed in a broader way than it is in Article 5.

A review of the differences between the levels of protection offered by the Constitution and the Convention shows the limitations of an interpretative model of incorporation. In order for individuals to have the maximum benefit of rights protection, it would be necessary for the Convention at least to have parity with the Constitution. Otherwise, the more limited constitutional definition of family would prevail, for example. The Constitution Review Group recognised the difference in levels of protection, in recommending that if incorporation were to take place, it should be done on a selective basis, with Convention rights replacing only those constitutional rights that offer inferior protection. This approach would at least ensure the retention of those constitutional rights offering superior protection. However, given the evolving jurisprudence of both the Strasbourg and the domestic courts, it would be difficult to predict with any degree of certainty which provisions would offer stronger protection in practice.

## The Irish Constitution and Human Rights

Whatever model of incorporation is adopted, some guidance for the future application of Convention rights in domestic law may be discerned in the way in which the Irish courts have interpreted constitutional rights. Despite sixty years of rights protection, it can be argued that the effect of constitutional rights in achieving improvement in the lives of ordinary people has been minimal. This is due in part to the type of belief-systems underlying the Constitution, and in part to the mostly conservative interpretation of the rights by judges.

The adoption of the 1937 Constitution involved the commitment by the state to guaranteeing a series of 'Fundamental Rights' contained in

Articles 40-44. These Articles adhere for the most part to the traditional civil-political model, with the individual having the right to take legal action to enforce binding rights to life, liberty, private property and freedom of religion, among others. By contrast, reference to economic and social rights is relegated to Article 45, the provision entitled 'Directive Principles of Social Policy', which as its title suggests does not bestow rights that are enforceable.

Article 45 of the Constitution expresses a commitment to ensuring that 'the ownership and control of the material resources of the community may be so distributed amongst private individuals and the various classes as best to subserve the common good', but this noble phrase has been largely ignored. No court has directly sought to hold the state to its pledge to 'safeguard with especial care the economic interests of the weaker sections of the community' nor to 'protect the public against unjust exploitation'.

The Constitution has failed to protect against poverty and its consequences, yet it could actively be used to challenge social exclusion. A minority of the Constitution Review Group argued that the Constitution could contain 'an Article committing us to a democracy based on principles of social solidarity with the aim of eliminating poverty and promoting economic equality through a system of taxation based on principles of equality and progressiveness'. However, a majority of the Group opposed the idea of specific protection of economic rights in the Constitution.

It is possible that economic rights may in the future be incorporated into the Irish Constitution, perhaps as the result of argument from a tradition of socialist political thought, or indeed from a Catholic perspective on social justice. Such a development might be seen as part of a process of reclaiming and invigorating the notion of rights. This is an optimistic view of future development, but one that nonetheless derives some support from the emergence of the international movement against neo-liberalism, with its adherence to a new philosophy of rights, based on principles of communitarianism and group justice. Signs of growing support for the idea of reclaiming rights are apparent in the September 1998 paper published by the Irish Commission for Justice and Peace on 'Re-Righting the Constitution', and in the Labour Party bill on economic and social rights, introduced in the Dáil in October 2000.

A fundamental change or re-evaluation of rights has already taken place once before, in the application of the constitutional rights provisions themselves. When they were first introduced, Articles 40-44 were a novelty, at odds with the concept of parliamentary supremacy with which the Irish judiciary had been trained. So for the first twenty-odd years after the enactment of the Constitution, the fundamental rights articles gave rise to little litigation. There were occasional judicial references to a higher law from which rights were said to derive, but it was not until the 1960s, with the arrival of a new generation of judges to the superior courts, that a clear change in approach came about.

The watershed year in terms of constitutional jurisprudence was 1963, with the Supreme Court decision in *Ryan v. Attorney General*, in which the plaintiff challenged legislation establishing a water fluoridation programme. Although there is no reference to any such right in the Constitution, the Supreme Court held that the right to bodily integrity is implicit in Article 40.3.1, which imposes a duty upon the

State to 'defend and vindicate the personal rights of the citizen'. Mr Justice Kenny held that this Article implicitly guarantees a range of other rights deriving from the 'Christian and democratic nature of the State', rather than from any express written clause. He invoked a Papal Encyclical in support of the right to bodily integrity, and referred to other unenumerated natural law rights, such as the right to marry and to free movement within the State.

The plaintiff in *Ryan* in fact lost her case since she had not actually established that water fluoridation was harmful to her health. Despite this, the *Ryan* decision marked the start of a period of extensive development of the 'natural law' doctrine of interpretation, whereby the Courts invoked Article 40.3.1, in conjunction with other Articles, in order to imply rights such as the right to earn a livelihood, the right to fair procedures, and the right to independent domicile. In *McGee v. Attorney General*, for example, legislation prohibiting contraceptives was successfully challenged on the grounds that it interfered with the implied constitutional right to marital privacy, again derived from Article 40.3.1.

The 1970s are now seen as the heyday of judicial activism, and a period in which life was certainly breathed into the hitherto under-used fundamental rights articles. But this activism had a shaky foundation, and at times it appeared as if judges were simply drawing rights out of the air. No consistent principles underscored the invocation of natural law principles. While some judges made clear that they believed the source of natural rights to be theological, derived from Christian or more particularly Catholic teaching, as expressed in Papal Encyclicals, other judges gave little indication as to their source of 'natural' rights.

When judges began to re-evaluate the rights provisions by taking this more activist approach, two contradictory philosophies emerged as influencing their interpretation of rights. On the one hand, the Constitution is clearly committed to the political ideology of liberalism, with its emphasis on the civil and political rights of the individual. Quinn (1989) argues, however, that another political ideology may also be discerned within it: that of theocracy. While liberal-democracy favours the autonomy of the individual, theocracy inclines towards the collective rights of the group. Theocracy bestows rights on the patriarchal family, whereas the emphasis in liberal-democratic theory is on the individual. During the heyday of judicial activism, theocracy was the more dominant ideology, with judges referring to Encyclicals to support their invocation of rights. More recently, theocracy has become marginalised, perhaps due to increased economic prosperity and greater acceptance of a market-generated philosophy of individualism. The resulting change towards a more classically liberal interpretation of the Constitution has meant greater emphasis on the rights of the individual.

Thus, the invocation of natural rights began to wane in the 1980s, and finally appeared to fall out of judicial favour in the 1995 *Regulation of Information Bill* decision, where the Supreme Court upheld the constitutionality of legislation providing for conditions under which information on abortion could be provided. In the course of argument in the case, it was suggested by counsel opposing the constitutionality of the Bill that it was repugnant to the Constitution since it was in conflict with natural law.

This meant that the Supreme Court was faced for the first time with the express question of whether natural law was superior to the

Constitution. The Court held that natural law cannot take priority over the text of the Constitution, since it represents the will of the people and is the supreme law in the State. The decision was described as heralding the 'death of natural law', but while natural law is certainly less frequently invoked by judges now, it remains the case that judges may still have reference to 'higher law' principles in order to assist with constitutional interpretation in occasional cases. So for example, in *Re a Ward of Court*, a case decided just two months after the *Regulation of Information Bill* decision, the Supreme Court held that a gastronomy tube could be removed from a woman patient who had been in a near-persistent vegetative state for 22 years. In coming to this decision, members of the Court referred to religious principles. Mrs Justice Denham, for example, supported a view expressed in an earlier case by Mr Justice Walsh that the Constitution 'reflects a firm conviction that we are a religious people'. Thus, she held that the interpretation of the right to life can be inclusive of a spiritual or religious component, but that this does not mean that life must always be prolonged: 'To care for the dying . . . and to free them from suffering rather than simply to postpone death, is to have fundamental respect for the sanctity of life and its end.'

In other words, although natural law theories no longer have the influence over judicial interpretation of the Constitution that they once did, it would be inaccurate to suggest that contemporary constitutional interpretation comprises an exclusively secular approach. Rather, it appears that natural law doctrine may continue to have some bearing on future superior courts' decisions. The effect of the development of natural law doctrine by the judiciary, with the potential for continued use of higher law principles to invalidate legislation, has been to give judges a great deal more power than the framers of the Constitution might have intended. The personal prejudices of individual judges have been reflected in their legal decisions, particularly when they are ruling on controversial topics. For example, Chief Justice O'Higgins in the 1984 *Norris* case described homosexuality as 'unnatural sexual conduct which Christian teaching held to be gravely sinful'; thankfully, not a view widely held today.

The use of interpretations favouring one sector of the community, that from which members of the judiciary are largely drawn, is another danger to which such unrestrained interpretative powers can lead. The danger of selective interpretation is particularly evident in relation to particular issues. Decisions on the freedom of association in Article 40.6.1(iii), for instance, have invariably been decided in favour of employers, or individual employees, against trade unions, so that attempts to use the provision to further collective rights have generally failed. A similar interpretative bias may be detected in relation to other Articles, and is perhaps most apparent in the jurisprudence relating to gender equality and to the rights of the family.

## Equality in the Constitution

The equality guarantee in Article 40.1 reads: 'All citizens shall, as human persons, be held equal before the law.' Even during the heyday of judicial activism, this guarantee has consistently been interpreted in a cautious and restrictive manner. Of all the fundamental rights provisions, it has had perhaps the least impact in litigation, partly because it is based on a limited concept of formal equality, which imposes only a negative duty of non-discrimination upon the state. This concept may be contrasted with that of substantive equality, which is based not upon sameness but upon difference. A state that is committed to ensuring substantive equality will recognise that, as the US Supreme Court has held, 'sometimes the greatest discrimination can lie in treating things that are different as though they were exactly alike.' The 'difference' argument therefore recognises the need to ensure that facially neutral laws do not impact in a discriminatory fashion upon certain groups, by virtue of their pre-existing differences.

Another reason for the limited effect of the guarantee lies in the proviso to the Article, which allows the state to have regard to 'differences of capacity, physical and moral, and of social function'. The phrase 'social function' is especially limiting in relation to gender equality when read together with Article 41.2 of the Constitution, which provides that 'by her life within the home, woman gives to the State a support without which the common good cannot be achieved'. The same Article commits the state to 'endeavour to ensure that mothers shall not be obliged by economic necessity to engage in labour to the neglect of their duties in the home.'

Despite numerous calls for the removal of this article from the Constitution, it remains in place, and indeed has been used on occasion to justify continued discriminations both against women and men, especially when read in conjunction with the 'social function' proviso. Thus, the courts have accepted as justified discrimination against an unmarried person as compared with a married person, and a man as compared with a woman in terms of the prohibition on homosexuality.

Even in those few cases where plaintiffs have successfully claimed discrimination, the courts have been reluctant to base decisions solely upon the equality guarantee. In *de Burca*, where legislation exempting women from jury service was struck down as unconstitutional, some of the judges based their reasoning upon the guarantee of trial by jury in Article 38.5. Similarly, in the *Murphy* case, in which a married couple successfully challenged a tax law which discriminated in favour of co-habiting couples, the Supreme Court held that the relevant legislation did not offend Article 40.1, because differences of social function existed between married and co-habiting couples. Instead, the legislature had breached Article 41.3.1 by failing to guard with special care the institution of marriage.

The constitutional equality guarantee aside, Irish legislation offers extensive protection against discrimination through the Employment Equality Act, 1998 and the Equal Status Act, 2000. Unfortunately both Acts, like Article 40.1, are based upon the concept of formal equality; little provision is made for positive action, and again enforcement will depend upon individuals taking claims against employers, clubs or other establishments, since few positive duties are imposed upon employers, service providers or the state. A slightly more radical version of the legislation was struck down earlier by the Supreme Court, on the basis that imposing duties on employers to reasonably accommodate persons with disabilities amounted to an interference with the employers' right to make profit. Thus, as Power (2000) writes, the equality guarantee was 'trumped' by the right to private property.

Under the new Acts, protection now exists against discrimination both in the workplace and in relation to the provision of goods and services on nine specified grounds: gender, marital and family status, sexual orientation, religion, age, disability, race and membership of the travelling community. The addition of new grounds is very welcome, since it provides a remedy against discrimination to groups such as Travellers who have long suffered discrimination and structural disadvantage in Irish society.

However, little provision is made in the new legislation for measures aimed at giving preference to any particular disadvantaged group, and the Acts contain significant exclusionary provisions. The employment legislation still allows religious-run medical and educational institutions to discriminate on the basis of religion in order to retain their religious ethos, and this has been subject to strong criticism by teachers' unions. The equal status law allows service providers, such as publicans, to refuse service where they reasonably believe that the provision of services would create a substantial risk of criminal or disorderly conduct or damage to property. Thus, where a pub-owner has a pub full of members of a racist group, he or she could legitimately refuse to serve a black customer on the grounds that the other customers present might create disorder in the pub as a result. This provision may undermine significantly the purpose of the Act.

Despite these and other flaws in the Acts, their introduction is highly significant for Irish society. For the first time, the concept of equality has been extended beyond the workplace to the marketplace, and protection against discrimination is afforded on much wider grounds than before. With some imagination, and creative use of the legislation, it may be possible to develop a genuinely effective equality policy that is not premised on outdated views of the 'social function' of different groups within our society. This may, however, take some time, and the Constitution in its present form is unlikely to be of much assistance in furthering the concept of equality.

## Gender equality: reproductive rights

In respect of gender equality, it is clear that legislation is leading the way, and that the Constitution has been particularly unsatisfactory, given its recognition of an outdated role for women in the home. However, in another respect the Constitution has devalued even more significantly the role of women. Following the 1983 Amendment, Article 40.3.3 was inserted into the Constitution, declaring that the right to life of the foetus is equal to the right to life of the pregnant woman. This Amendment has had a profound effect for the rights and status of women within Irish society; Ireland is now the only EU member state in which abortion is unlawful in all but the most extreme circumstances. But in fact the Irish abortion rate is comparable to that of any other European country, since thousands of Irish women each year travel to England to obtain legal abortions there.

The 1983 Amendment generated a series of cases in which the courts held that the provision of information on abortion was in breach of the Constitution, since it undermined the right to life of the foetus. Ultimately, in 1993 the European Court of Human Rights found that the actions of the Irish State in effectively prohibiting the dissemination of information on abortion were in breach of Article 10 of the Convention, which guarantees the right to freedom of expression. Further, in a reference of the same issue by a group of students' unions to the European Court of Justice, that Court raised the possibility that a future right to provide information on abortion might be established through EC law, defining abortion as a 'service' within the meaning of the Treaty of Rome.

The result of the interpretations offered by various courts as to the implications of Article 40.3.3 for information on abortion might be described as unexpected. However, the second line of authority, relating to the issue of abortion itself, has produced an equally unexpected result, although it should have been predictable that where the rights of pregnant woman and foetus come into conflict, the courts would inevitably have to decide which take priority. Such a situation arose in two cases in the 1990s, the *X* and the *C* case, both involving young girls pregnant as a result of rape. The two rights were decided by the courts to be in conflict in each case, due to the suicidal intentions expressed by both X and C arising from their crisis pregnancies.

It was accepted by the Supreme Court in the *X* case, in the words of Chief Justice Finlay, that if 'there is a real and substantial risk to the life, as distinct from the health, of the mother, which can only be avoided by the termination of her pregnancy, such termination is permissible.' The *X* case decision, followed in *C*, has the effect of rendering abortion lawful where necessary to save the life of the pregnant woman. It should be noted that although the word 'mother' is used in the Constitution, 'pregnant woman' is more accurate, since many women who have abortions are not mothers, and some are still children.

Following the *X* and *C* decisions, the All-Party Oireachtas Committee on the Constitution produced a report on abortion law in November 2000. While no firm conclusion was reached by the members of the committee, a minority favoured another referendum to restrict the effect of the *X* case judgement, so that abortion would only be lawful in circumstances where the risk to the woman's health was physical. Risk of suicide would no longer be a ground for termination. Such a referendum, if adopted, would have a very dangerous effect. The *X* case represents the most limited form of abortion possible — that necessary to save the life of the woman — so any restriction of the test case would endanger the lives of pregnant women, particularly those at risk of suicide.

It is not appropriate that abortion should be regulated through the Constitution at all, given the oppositional nature of constitutional rights. Rather, Article 40.3.3 of the Constitution should ultimately be repealed, given the complications which have arisen as to its interpretation, and given the status to which it demotes women, equating them with the potential life in their wombs. The regulation of abortion through a legislative framework, permitting abortion on request, is the only way in which the control by women of their fertility will be assured.

Feminists have argued for abortion itself to be seen as a human right, since the extent to which women exercise control over their fertility affects their choices in every aspect of their lives: their participation in employment, education and training, in the household and local community and in the wider political and public spheres. There is an emerging argument that abortion may be framed in terms of an international human right, by reference to the Convention on the Elimination of All Forms of Discrimination Against Women (CEDAW), the only international treaty to mention family planning.

This argument has not influenced the jurisprudence of the Strasbourg Court, however, and it has never ruled directly on the question of whether a ban on abortion is compatible with the Convention. It could be argued that a right to abortion under the Convention could be identified through the guarantees of personal liberty or of equality, but its recognition in an Irish context appears to be a long way off. One could argue that the retention of Article 40.3.3 in the Constitution represents a bastion of theocratic ideology, a stand taken against the onset of full-blown liberalism with its attendant emphasis on individual liberties and thus the potential for recognition of a liberty-based right to abortion. The interpretation of Article 40.3.3 by the judiciary in the *X* and *C* cases, however, shows a break with theocratic ideology, and a judicial impatience with legislative inaction, in the use of harmonious interpretation to justify finding in favour of each girl's right to life.

## The Rights of the Family

Theocracy is still alive and well as an ideology in the application of Article 41 of the Constitution, which guarantees the rights of the family, recognising it as 'the natural primary and fundamental unit group of society . . . a moral institution possessing inalienable and imprescriptible rights, antecedent and superior to all positive law.' This Article, framed in absolutist language, has been interpreted in order to preserve a particularly conservative definition of the 'family', limited to the family based upon marriage. In 1965, the Supreme Court ruled in *Nicolaou*'s case that the father of a non-marital child had no right to prevent the mother from giving the child up for adoption, since he was not part of a constitutionally protected family. This decision was followed in 1980 when the

Supreme Court held further that an unmarried mother and her child did not constitute a family in the sense of Article 41.

In other judgments, the courts have reinforced the distinction between the constitutionally protected marital family and other groups, who may define themselves as family, but do not attract the same constitutional protection. In *W.O'R v. E.H.*, the Supreme Court was asked in 1996 whether the concept of *de facto* family was recognised in the Constitution, but emphatically rejected that notion. Chief Justice Hamilton distinguished the Irish approach from Strasbourg Court jurisprudence, in which the rights of non-marital families under Article 8 have been expressly upheld; in *Keegan*'s case, for example.

Despite the limitations of the Constitution, legislation has again hugely improved the lot of women and children within the family. The Status of Children Act 1987 abolished the status of illegitimacy; the Judicial Separation and Family Law Reform Act 1989 allowed the courts to take into account each spouse's contribution to the family in allocating property on marriage breakdown. Legislation now allows those not in marital relationships to seek protection against violence in the home. Most significantly, in 1995 Article 41 was amended by referendum to allow divorce legislation to be enacted. Incorporation of the Convention could improve further the protection of those outside of the marital family structure, and might encourage the Irish judiciary to take a more inclusive view of 'family'.

## An activist judiciary?

Although the courts tend to apply restrictive interpretations to constitutional guarantees of equality and of family rights, there are still areas in which judicial activism is apparent, despite the fall into disfavour of natural law theory. Indeed, the judiciary has had a significant role in shaping recent policy in two particular areas: immigration law, and the care of children with special needs.

Court decisions have had a major impact on immigration and asylum policy. In the *Fajujonu* case, the Court relied upon the Article 41 rights of the family in ruling that where a married couple were residing illegally in the state, but had children born in the state who were therefore Irish citizens, those children as citizens had a constitutional right to the 'company, care and parentage of their parents within a family unit'. This decision has meant in practice that many of those asylum-seekers or others who would not otherwise be legally entitled to remain in Ireland may assert an entitlement to reside by virtue of their children's family rights. Its effect has been further strengthened by the provision of the Good Friday Agreement entitling all of those born on the island of Ireland to Irish citizenship. As a result, it has become, quite correctly, very difficult to deport the non-national parents of an Irish citizen. An even more dramatic result was caused by *Laurentiu*'s case, where the Court found sections of the Aliens Act, 1935 to be unconstitutional as vesting legislative powers in the executive, so that hundreds of deportation orders were invalidated and deportations themselves were suspended for most of a year.

Thus, judicial decisions have had significant effect upon legislative policy on asylum and immigration matters, which itself is widely regarded as shambolic and lacking in fair procedures. Thousands of persons seeking refugee status under the Geneva Convention procedures have waited years to be processed through a creaking and inadequate asylum processing system, yet there is a lack of any proper immigration policy for those who come here to work, rather than to flee persecution. Recent legislation has compounded the injustice of the way in which asylum applications are processed.

In particular, the Illegal Immigrants (Trafficking) Bill, 2000, upheld by the Supreme Court, imposes strict time limits on the review of asylum decisions, and allows for detention for up to eight weeks of those against whom deportation orders have been made. Yet the Supreme Court held that its provisions were not in breach either of the Constitution or of the Convention, in accepting that detention under the Bill did not amount to preventive detention, but rather detention for the purpose of implementing a deportation order. This distinction can best be described as artificial, since the purpose of such detention is really to prevent the detainee from avoiding the carrying-out of the deportation order. The effect of the judgment is unfortunate, in that it bolsters an unjust and inadequate asylum policy generated as much by the Executive as by the Legislature.

In the area of litigation on behalf of children with special needs, however, judges have retained a high degree of activism in a series of cases since 1980, mostly taken under Article 42 (the right to education). The courts have played a pivotal role in securing rights for disadvantaged children and children with disabilities, challenging inexcusable legislative failures. In the 1980 decision of *G v. An Bord Uchtala*, Mr Justice Finlay held that a child has a constitutional right to bodily integrity and an 'unenumerated right to an opportunity to be reared with due regard to her religious, moral, intellectual, physical and social welfare'. In the *FN* case in 1995, Mr Justice Geogheghan held there was a constitutional obligation on the state under Article 42.5 to vindicate the rights of a child with hyperkinetic conduct disorder who required a period of time in a secure unit.

In the crucial case of *O'Donoghue,* one year later, the Supreme Court strengthened significantly the protection owed by the state to children, ruling that a boy with a profound learning disability was entitled to free primary education in accordance with Article 42.4, and that the state was thus obliged to provide him with the supports necessary to enable him to receive his entitlement. More recently, a similar decision was made in respect of *Sinnott,* a case involving an adult with severe learning disability.

Apart from children with disabilities, the courts have also been active in securing the rights of children suffering severe disadvantage, particularly in situations where the parents are unable to provide for them and existing state supports have proved inadequate. In *DB,* the case of a 15-year-old applicant who required secure accommodation for his own welfare, Mr Justice Kelly in the High Court gave a landmark 1998 judgment injuncting the Minister for Health to 'provide sufficient funding to allow the Eastern Health Board to build, open and maintain a 24-bed high support unit at Portrane in the County of Dublin'. In this, he went further than previous judges had done in granting a mandatory order against the state.

More recently, in the case of a 17-year-old girl deemed to be a danger to herself and others, the same judge went further, in imposing an order directing the three relevant Ministers personally to provide secure accommodation for the child. The order was only in place for a number of days before provision was made for the child by an Executive reeling from the shock of this drastic action. If the Ministers had not complied with the order, the suggestion was that Mr Justice Kelly would take the next step of imprisoning them for contempt of court.

While the Ministers escaped prison on this occasion, this order and previous decisions of the same judge have been subject to criticism on the basis that it should not be the function of the courts to formulate educational or childcare policy. The childcare decisions certainly go beyond the traditional role of the judiciary in directing the Executive to provide facilities for children at risk. However, it can be argued that judges had little alternative in these cases where the state had effectively been on notice for years as to its duty to minors exhibiting problems, and yet had patently failed to take the necessary steps to meet their needs.

The consequences of the childcare decisions have also been criticised. In effect, the courts are really now determining how resources in childcare are to be expended. Of necessity, they are being directed at the building of high-support and secure units for the most troubled children, which are thus being prioritised at the expense of the equally important early intervention family supports advocated by many frontline social workers. The focus is on containing those children most at risk; but a more long-term policy should be directed at preventing any children from getting to the stage of needing high-support secure units. Early intervention is the preferable approach, but the courts cannot be blamed for the failure of the Executive to develop a policy based on early intervention in time. While children needing extreme levels of care are coming before the courts, the courts have a duty to ensure that their rights are vindicated.

It is noteworthy that the right to education, the only constitutionally guaranteed right not fitting within the civil and political mould, should continue to generate case-law imposing serious duties of expenditure upon the state, at a time when judicial activism is less marked than it was previously.  In short, these decisions, and the controversy over the large number of cases involving children at risk presently before the courts, have fuelled debate about the role of judicial activism. They have raised questions about the separation of powers doctrine itself, questions which will become more relevant with the incorporation of the Convention and the attendant additional powers that will be conferred upon the judiciary.

## Human Rights protection and the separation of powers doctrine

According to classic statements of the separation of powers doctrine, the Legislature alone makes law, the Executive implements law, and the Judiciary must interpret and apply law. This principle is enshrined in Article 15.2.1 of the Irish Constitution: 'The sole and exclusive power of making laws for the state is hereby vested in the Oireachtas.' There may be breaches of the doctrine in practice, but it is seen as essential to the functioning of a liberal democracy. Where the judiciary take on a lawmaking role, therefore, the doctrine is breached in a fundamental way. Where the power to make law is being left to judges, there is clearly a flaw in the workings of the Legislature. Members of the legislature, unlike judges, are elected and accountable. It is they who should be holding the Government to task over the failure to enact legislation on abortion, over the failure to provide an adequate immigration policy, or an effective policy meeting the needs of children at risk. Instead, legislative inactivity tends to thrust a lawmaking role upon judges and can endanger the workings of democracy.

Another danger is that judicial subjectivism may thus become enshrined as law. When the majority of our judges are drawn from a homogenous class background then, no matter how fair-minded they are as individuals, their judgments may reflect a view of society not shared by those upon whom their decisions will most impact.

On the other hand, judicial lawmaking can also be seen in a positive light. Judges in a country with a written constitution have a strong protective role against legislative or executive abuse of power, and of course against legislative inaction. Vitally important judicial decisions have re-defined and strengthened democracy in our system. The decision on the Single European Act in *Crotty* established the need to hold a referendum on entry into international obligations impacting on national sovereignty; the decision arising out of the divorce referendum in *McKenna* resulted in a fundamental re-think about the way in which referendum campaigns are run. In Ireland it could well be argued that judges have asserted popular sovereignty where both Legislature and Executive have notably failed.

The Irish legal system could be described as operating on a compromise basis, with lawmaking powers vested in the Oireachtas, supplemented by some residual judicial lawmaking to hold the legislators in check and shore up individual rights in cases of policy failure. But this can result in uneasy and unsatisfactory compromise, with a strong element of uncertainty, and with tension between the legislative and judicial functions. It is also a compromise that does not ultimately make for good or effective policies in difficult areas where democratic debate, conducted through the Legislature, is needed in order to achieve a more adequate resolution of issues.

## Conclusion

It appears, from this necessarily brief consideration of the extent to which a 'human rights culture' exists, that we have not really measured up as a society even to protecting those limited civil and political rights guaranteed in our constitutional bill of rights. While incorporation of the Convention is certainly to be welcomed for its symbolic value and its part in furthering the peace process, one might be cynical about the practical effect of incorporation of the Convention into Irish law. It would be reasonable to conclude that it is unlikely to generate a human rights culture, or to really change things for people.

To some extent, the merits of this conclusion depend on the method of incorporation chosen. The Convention would have little effect if incorporated according to the interpretation model, since constitutional rights would remain pre-eminent. Even if it was incorporated in a more meaningful way, however, it could only generate limited change. In a number of areas, such as privacy and family rights, freedom of expression, and the rights of those accused of criminal offences, it might alter the results of individual cases. But since it encompasses the same package of rights already given constitutional protection through Irish domestic law, it is unlikely to have any extensive impact, however incorporated, and certainly unlikely to generate a 'culture of rights'.

The experience in the past of failures in the separation of powers doctrine does not bode well for the development of a human rights culture, either. With the absence of principled or ideological debate in the Legislature, and the reluctance by politicians to take on difficult issues, the judiciary have been left to step into the vacuum thus created. In some instances, they have been forced to create policy in areas neglected by those charged with making law. In other areas, judicial subjectivism dressed in a cloak of 'natural law' principles has been very apparent. Yet these tensions between the arms of government are likely to be exacerbated by the incorporation of the Convention. Whatever type of human rights regime is in place, a more effectively functioning Legislature is needed to facilitate principled political debate.

Through such debate, it might ultimately be possible to generate a genuine human rights culture, through the development of a new conception of rights, based on an economic and social model. The dynamism of new anti-corporatist movements internationally and the arguments that have been made here for a change in rights-thought can provide a basis from which to progress this changed vision. Otherwise, even with the best rights-enforcement machinery in the world, the limited guarantees of civil and political rights can at best improve only the lot of individuals, not of disadvantaged classes or groups. Before a new human rights culture can emerge, a new concept of human rights must be developed.

# Human Rights in Northern Ireland: In from the Margins?

STEPHEN LIVINGSTONE

## Introduction

As the authors of one article on human rights after the Belfast Agreement put it, the last few years have witnessed a move 'from the margins to the mainstream' of human rights issues in relation to the Northern Ireland conflict. For much of the past thirty years human rights issues have never been far away from the surface of the Northern Ireland conflict, with repeated claims that both the state and its opponents were involved in significant levels of human rights violations. However, little was done to respond to this. At times debates over human rights appeared simply to become part of a depressing cycle of claim and counter-claim between supporters and opponents of the status quo. The latter argued that human rights violations undermined the State's authority while the former replied that those who had infringed the most fundamental right of all, the right to life, were scarcely in a position to lecture anyone on human rights. Efforts to advance the argument that everyone in Northern Ireland had certain rights that should be respected, and that the challenge was to identify means of ensuring that they were effectively respected, were essentially bypassed.

However, since 1998 all this appears to have changed. The Agreement itself is replete with phrases about respecting the rights of all and how they should become the foundation of a new society. It has given rise to a new institution, the Northern Ireland Human Rights Commission (NIHRC), which is charged with a range of functions to better advance the cause of human rights in Northern Ireland, as well as a sister institution for the Republic of Ireland. The two major commissions of inquiry established by the Belfast Agreement, the Patten Commission and the Criminal Justice Review, have both pronounced respect for human rights to be at the centre of their recommendations. The Human Rights Act, 1998 has incorporated fundamental rights into Northern Irish law for the first time and the Northern Ireland Act, 1998 gives these rights an almost constitutional status by providing that the Assembly does not have the competence to make legislation inconsistent with them. The range of rights protected may be further extended beyond the UK-wide provisions of the Human Rights Act by a specific Bill of Rights for Northern Ireland, on which the NIHRC has already begun to consult. The language of human rights is increasingly being appropriated and used by statutory agencies, political parties and voluntary organisations throughout Northern Ireland.

This paper welcomes these developments and takes as its premise the idea that respect for the rights of all is indeed crucial to dealing with the causes of conflict in Northern Ireland. However, it goes on to argue that there remain a number of unresolved problems and questions regarding effective respect for human rights in Northern Ireland, which widespread mouthing of the mantra of the need to respect human rights may serve only to mask rather than answer. Some of these have to do with the question of what human rights it is that we are seeking to protect. The development of international human rights law over the past 50 years has offered a wide range of standards which states may seek to give effect to in their national law. Although the standards of the European Convention on Human Rights have been given effect to through the Human Rights Act and the Northern Ireland Act, there remains a widespread perception that more is needed in Northern Ireland, though exactly what that more is remains disputed. A second set of issues relates to potential points of resistance in Northern Ireland. Taking rights seriously will involve a challenge to the power and mode of operation of a number of institutions. It remains to be seen where such resistance will come from and whether those advocating the cause of human rights do indeed have sufficient resources to overcome it.

This paper seeks to explore these issues in greater depth, to examine what sort of human rights regime may evolve for Northern Ireland and what resistances it might face. Before doing so, however, it will examine briefly the history of how we got to our current position and what influence the themes identified in this history might exercise on future developments.

## Human Rights in the Years of Conflict

Initially, of course, the issue of human rights was very much to the fore in the present phase of the Northern Ireland conflict. At that time it was better known as Civil Rights, under which banner a widespread but short-lived coalition of interests sought change in Northern Ireland. The civil rights movement of the mid and late 1960s, which drew significant inspiration from comparable developments in the United States, pushed above all for equality rights, notably in the spheres of voting, housing and public employment. Allied to these was a broad range of other civil rights claims, notably to free expression, free assembly and fairness in the criminal justice system, which crystallised in demands for the repeal of the Special Powers Acts, 1922-33.

Many of the equality demands were to be accepted, at least in principle, by the mid 1970s. By that time Northern Ireland had already descended into a period of violent conflict in which issues of human rights became increasingly marginalised. Although the Special Powers Act was repealed in 1972, it was immediately replaced by the Emergency Provisions Act, 1973 which gave similarly wide powers of search, arrest and detention to the police and now extended most of these to the military. These powers were subsequently built upon by the Prevention of Terrorism Act, 1974, which arguably institutionalised such powers more effectively by extending them to the whole of the United Kingdom. Far from declining, allegations of human rights abuses rose sharply from the early 1970s onwards and began to include claims of especially grave breaches of human rights such as arbitrary killing, torture, detention without trial and miscarriages of justice. Yet government, now the Westminster government that had taken over responsibility under direct rule, became arguably less willing to hear such concerns. Although some changes were made to strengthen protection of human rights, notably the creation of a Standing Advisory Commission on Human Rights (SACHR) in 1973, the passing of a law on religious discrimination in employment and a number of reforms on police accountability, more fundamental change was blocked on the grounds that it would only assist the activities of terrorists.

Some of these draconian laws were supported by those who once marched for civil rights, on the grounds that terrorism now posed the more fundamental threat to the rights of all. In the more polarised atmosphere of Northern Ireland in the 1970s, others lost their interest in the advocacy of human rights as this was seen as too reformist a strategy. Its focus on extending 'British' rights to Northern Ireland seemed to some little more than a way of reinforcing partition, and powerless to deal with significant problems arising in Ireland.

By the early 1980s, therefore, advocacy of human rights in relation to Northern Ireland was in fairly bad shape. Once-powerful local organisations, such as the Northern Ireland Civil Rights Association and the Association for Legal Justice, had effectively collapsed through internal division and apathy. The Standing Advisory Commission on Human Rights constantly lacked the financial resources and frequently lacked the quality of personnel to make an impact; moreover, even its modest recommendations were largely ignored by government. Civil liberties organisations in Britain and Ireland, with the notable exception of the National Council for Civil Liberties (now Liberty) in London, largely lacked the capacity or will to become involved in an issue which only threatened to divide them and rob them of the support they had built up on less contentious matters.

Only international human rights organisations, notably Amnesty International, were able to offer sustained and independent human rights criticism of the government's human rights record. As a result of an Amnesty investigation into Castlereagh detention centre in 1978, the government was compelled to hold an inquiry and make significant changes in the regime for those interrogated under emergency powers.

However, for the most part government was able to deflect such international criticism, for example allegations of arbitrary killings by the security forces, by pointing to the virulence of the terrorist campaign being waged against those security forces and the ordinary people of Northern Ireland. Even efforts to raise the profile of equality issues in the United States, perhaps the most significant human rights initiative relating to Northern Ireland for most of the 1980s, were largely resisted by the government as being a sop to terrorists. While some political parties in Northern Ireland maintained a call for greater protection of human rights throughout this period, this could also be dismissed as simply resorting to another stick with which to beat the government, devoid of a general commitment to protecting the rights of all.

Two things in particular were to change this situation from the mid 1980s onwards and begin the rise of human rights to the prominence it enjoys today. The first was the Anglo-Irish Agreement of 1985. Central to the Agreement was a recognition that human rights abuses had played a significant role in alienating northern nationalists from the state. The Agreement did not include any explicit commitments to change laws or practices inimical to human rights, but it did acknowledge the legitimacy of the Irish government raising human rights issues relating to Northern Ireland with the UK government, and provide a number of means (such as consultation on the membership of SACHR) whereby the Irish government could influence the human rights agenda relating to Northern Ireland. It also provided the Irish government with a channel through which it could regularly raise human rights issues. This channel in turn helped to empower human rights non-governmental organisations (NGOs) who began to feed information and concerns to the Irish government as a means of ensuring they would be more forcefully raised with the British government than the NGOs themselves could do.

More broadly, the Agreement marked a recognition that tackling concerns about abuses of human rights was crucial to dealing with the conflict in Northern Ireland and that the UK government could not simply dismiss such criticism as the propaganda of those hostile to the state. This clearly did not mean an end to concern about human rights violations — indeed some of the most controversial incidents relating to the use of lethal force and alleged collusion have arisen since 1985 — but it did mark a change in the character of official discourse relating to them. Joint British-Irish statements from 1985 onwards increasingly referred to matters of human rights in relation to Northern Ireland.

The second motivator, perhaps less obvious, was the end of the Cold War. This liberated human rights at the international level from a significant straitjacket that had impeded their development. From the late 1980s onwards we have witnessed a significant growth of international human rights law and institutions, both inter-governmental and non-governmental, which seek to ensure its enforcement. This growth has impacted on Northern Ireland in a number of ways. Local human rights organisations, notably the Committee on the Administration of Justice (CAJ), increasingly adopted international human rights provisions as the standard by which to evaluate the actions of the state. Since advocating respect for such standards could not be said to be simply a call to see 'British' or 'Irish' justice enforced, human rights advocacy was no longer trapped in a reformist/revolutionary dilemma.

An increasing range of other organisations, including political parties across the spectrum, has been able to take up this call to see international human rights standards given effect.

A second impact of the developments at the international level has been that a range of international institutions, encouraged by groups such as the CAJ or British Irish Rights Watch, have taken a greater interest in human rights issues in Northern Ireland. Throughout the years of conflict, applications from Northern Ireland went to the European Commission and Court of Human Rights in Strasbourg. Sensitive to the terrorist threat which faced many western European States for much of the 1970s and 1980s, that institution has in the past been perhaps too willing to allow the United Kingdom a broad 'margin of appreciation' as regards the conformity of its anti-terrorist policies with human rights standards. However, in the last ten years a series of rulings on arrest powers, the right to silence, confessions and the use of lethal force have all added credence to the view that human rights have not been fully respected in Northern Ireland. Moreover other international institutions began to take an interest in Northern Ireland from the early 1990s onwards, institutions which either had not existed or had little to say on the issue in the previous two decades. The European Committee on the Prevention of Torture, after its first visit to Northern Ireland in 1993, indicated a view that conditions in Castlereagh Holding Centre gave rise to a significant risk of inhuman and degrading treatment and recommended that the Centre should be closed. The United Nations Committee on Torture also expressed concern throughout the 1990s regarding the treatment of detainees in police detention, while both its Sub Commission on

Human Rights and its Special Rapporteur on the Independence of Judges and Lawyers were to draw attention to lack of government action in respect of threats to lawyers.

In addition to these international inter-governmental organisations, a variety of international human rights NGOs also began to take a greater interest in the affairs of Northern Ireland from the late 1980s onwards. While Amnesty International has always maintained a strong interest in Northern Ireland, regularly initiating missions and publishing reports on allegations of torture or state killings, it is only in the last decade that other international human rights NGOs have become more significantly involved. Prominent among these are the US-based Human Rights Watch and the Lawyers Committee for Human Rights, which have intervened on issues such as the policing of demonstrations, children's rights and threats to lawyers. Like Amnesty, these organisations have also extended their investigations to look at the activities of non-governmental groups and have been critical of both loyalist and republican groups, notably for their involvement in kidnapping, torture and extrajudicial executions. The reports of Amnesty, Human Rights Watch and the Lawyers Committee have been especially influential in the United States, where the issue of human rights violations in Northern Ireland was taken up with increasing vigour at both legislative and executive level in the years of the Clinton Presidency.

A greater international profile, pressure from the US and Irish governments, a rejuvenated local human rights lobby, a broader acceptance of international human rights standards throughout Northern Ireland and a recognition that human rights concerns had something to do with the causes of conflict made it likely that some reference to human rights would be made in any agreement. As we shall see, there is in fact quite a lot of reference to human rights in the Good Friday Agreement but in a way which still leaves the fate of human rights in Northern Ireland uncertain to a considerable degree.

## The Human Rights provisions of the Good Friday Agreement

Despite the developments outlined above, it does not seem that human rights was to the forefront of the minds of those who engaged in the multi-party talks from 1997 onwards. Issues about the arrangements for the new Executive and Assembly, their relationship to political institutions in Britain and Ireland, and the question of weapons no doubt loomed larger for the various political parties and governments involved. However, there also does seem to have been an acknowledgment that resolving the Northern Ireland conflict required not just an historic deal at the macro level between the representatives of the contending factions, but also new measures to build trust and confidence at the micro level. Nationalists in particular needed to see new measures in the human rights field lest the new institutions of government collapse and a security-orientated approach come to the fore again. Yet unionists also had an incentive to agree to new human rights provisions, both as a way of securing nationalist agreement to a solution falling short of Irish unity and as insurance to preserve their own rights to protest if Britain moved in the direction of joint authority.

However, the lower status of human rights concerns is reflected in the fact that, as several observers have attested, the human rights concerns only got into the Agreement at the later stages of drafting and they got there in a somewhat haphazard way. Thus the Agreement stops short of providing a comprehensive or even interim Bill of Rights on which to base the new dispensation on human rights, as happened in South Africa, for example. Instead there is a mixture of commitment to new laws, commitment to new institutions and even vaguer statements of principle. Most prominent among the new laws is the bringing into force of the Human Rights Act, 1998 and a new duty on public authorities to ensure equality of opportunity, which has subsequently borne fruit in Section 75 of the Northern Ireland Act, 1998. The Agreement also contains the commitment on the part of the Irish government to incorporate the European Convention on Human Rights into Irish law, something that has yet to occur, and enhanced equality legislation in the Republic, which has come to pass. Most prominent among the new institutions is the Northern Ireland Human Rights Commission (which replaces SACHR) and the Equality Commission for Northern Ireland (to replace the old Fair Employment Commission, Equal Opportunities Commission and Commission for Racial Equality, with new responsibility for disability discrimination also added in). A Human Rights Commission was also established, after a considerable delay, in the Republic. Although the establishment of commissions to look at policing and a criminal justice review in Northern Ireland were not explicitly included as part of the human rights aspects of the Agreement, each institution has subsequently put human rights at the heart of its recommendations.

The vaguer commitments include reference to a potential Charter of Rights for Ireland (to be devised by the Human Rights Commissions North and South), some measures on the Irish language and Ulster Scots (which could be seen as coming under the heading of cultural rights) and greater respect for the rights of victims. There is also a set of statements at the beginning of the 'Rights, Safeguards and Equality of Opportunity' Section of the Agreement indicating a commitment to the protection of the rights of all. These rights include the right to 'seek constitutional change by peaceful and legitimate means' and the right to 'freely choose one's place of residence', yet no indication is given as to whether they are currently adequately respected or how they might be given effect to in the future.

For those who feel that human rights have not been protected as well as they should have been in Northern Ireland, and that the failure to do so contributed to the development and extension of the conflict, such a plethora of references to human rights is indeed welcome. It is especially significant that the parties did not simply make a statement of the rights they felt were in need of respect but also provided specific commitments and created institutional forms to ensure their protection. However, the somewhat haphazard way in which these provisions have been assembled also provokes a certain degree of concern as to whether they amount to a human rights regime adequate to deal with the specific problems of Northern Ireland. For example, the European Convention on Human Rights (on which the Human Rights Act is based) is an impressive human rights instrument. However, as has already been alluded to, human rights lawyers in Northern Ireland have not always found its application to be satisfactory and it is being introduced to Northern Ireland largely because it is being introduced to the United Kingdom as a whole. Yet Northern Ireland has experienced human rights problems over the past thirty years rather different from those of England, Scotland and Wales.

Helpfully, a way to move beyond the European Convention is signalled in the Agreement itself. One of the tasks assigned to the new Northern Ireland Human Rights Commission is to advise the Secretary of State 'on the scope for including in Westminster legislation other rights supplemental to those contained in the European Convention on Human Rights'. The Commission's task in devising a Bill of Rights for Northern Ireland, on which it embarked in March 2000, provides an ideal opportunity for producing a more coherent framework on which to base the protection of human rights in Northern Ireland, and the ideal point at which to move from the past to consider the future for human rights in Northern Ireland.

## A Northern Ireland Bill of Rights

The key passage of the Agreement states:

> The new Northern Ireland Human Rights Commission . . . will be invited to consult and advise on the scope for defining, in Westminster legislation, rights supplementary to those in the European Convention on Human Rights, to reflect the particular circumstances of Northern Ireland, drawing as appropriate on international instruments and experience. These additional rights to reflect the principle of mutual respect for

the identity and ethos of both communities and parity of esteem, and — taken together with the ECHR — to constitute a Bill of Rights for Northern Ireland. Among issues for consideration by the Commission will be

- The formulation of a general obligation on government and public bodies fully to respect, on the basis of equality of treatment, the identity and ethos of both communities in Northern Ireland
- A clear formulation of the rights not to be discriminated against and to equality of opportunity in both the public and private sectors.

The obligation to advise the Secretary of State on a Bill of Rights provides a major opportunity but also a significant threat for the new Commission. The threat is that the Agreement does not commit the UK government or anyone else to having a Bill of Rights for Northern Ireland. Rather it, and Section 70 (7) of the Northern Ireland Act, 1998, merely commit the Northern Ireland Human Rights Commission to providing advice to the Secretary of State for Northern Ireland on the scope for such a Bill of Rights. There is no guarantee that the advice they provide will indicate the need for a Bill of Rights, or that the Secretary of State will take their advice. However, it has been clear from almost the first day of the Human Rights Commission's existence that its members do see the ECHR as a limited charter of rights and take the view that a stronger Bill of Rights for Northern Ireland is desirable. What is less clear is whether the Secretary of State is of the same opinion, though Peter Mandelson, then Secretary of State, welcomed the Commission's launch of its consultation process on the Bill of Rights and said that he looked forward to seeing what it will produce. It is unlikely that his successors or indeed any other Secretary of State will take action unless presented with a Bill of Rights which enjoys a wide consensus of public support. The threat for the NIHRC is that if they cannot achieve that consensus no Bill will be passed, putting them back in the position SACHR was for over twenty years as its calls to incorporate the ECHR fell on deaf ears.

However, if the threat is significant the opportunity is greater. The process of consulting on the content of a Bill of Rights offers the Commission a major opportunity for public education on the scope and meaning of human rights provisions. Beyond that, if the Commission can achieve public consensus on the content of the Bill of Rights then that document could serve as a major point of reference for a new Northern Ireland. Arguably for many people it could be even more significant than the Agreement. For while the Agreement relates mainly to arrangements between politicians and governments, the Bill of Rights relates directly to individuals and communities. It would be a statement not only of what rights every person sees as important to protect for themselves but also, since it is normally a condition of the existence of rights that they apply equally, what they see as important to protect for every other member of the society. Hence a Bill of Rights which enjoys widespread support and ownership has the potential to be a significant unifying symbol in a polity which has few of them.

What is the Bill of Rights to contain? The Agreement offers little guidance beyond the fact that it is to be additional to the ECHR and that it is to 'reflect the particular circumstances of Northern

Ireland'. The first causes few problems for human rights lawyers. The ECHR is now generally seen as a somewhat outdated human rights instrument. While it is strong on civil and political rights, as befits a document forged in the early days of the Cold War, it lacks most of the economic and social rights which are found in more recent human rights treaties. Human rights lawyers, notably the current UN High Commissioner, Mrs Mary Robinson, have increasingly stressed the 'indivisibility' of these two kinds of rights and of how ensuring the protection of rights to privacy or free expression, for example, depends on securing rights such as those to housing or adequate health care. The reverse is also true. Nor does the ECHR contain many of the rights focused on particularly vulnerable groups, such as children, minorities or victims, which have become increasingly prominent in international human rights law.

The Agreement also suggests that the Bill of Rights should reflect the particular circumstances of Northern Ireland. One interpretation I would argue against, though the Agreement leans in this direction and it might be the easiest approach to sell politically, is to limit this to 'two traditions' concerns through a beefed-up equality clause and some reference to equal respect for 'British' and 'Irish' language and culture. My reason for not going down this route is the awareness that while the conflict of nationalities may be the central division of Northern Ireland, many people would see their identity as being captured at best partially by these two categories. Protestants and Catholics may also see themselves as women, children, the elderly, homosexual or secularists. Other ethnic minorities may not be included by it at all. Indeed one might argue that such is the extensive protection given to the 'two communities' at a political level, through the power-sharing arrangements in the Assembly and Executive plus the North-South and East-West dimensions, that it is precisely these other identities which need greater protection in a Bill of Rights. Neglecting other forms of human rights abuse on the grounds that they are not 'specific to Northern Ireland' can have unwelcome consequences. Recent research on racial attitudes and prejudice in Northern Ireland indicated that over 30% of respondents were unwilling to accept someone from an ethnic minority as a work colleague and over 50% were unwilling to accept them as a close relative. One wonders if these percentages would have been as high had race discrimination legislation been introduced to Northern Ireland in 1976, as with the rest of the UK, and not 1997.

Some have taken the view that 'particular circumstances of Northern Ireland' is so vague as to be meaningless, and have seen this as giving them licence to advocate the incorporation of all the human rights standards the UK is party to, as well perhaps as some non-binding international provisions like the Code of Conduct for Law Enforcement Officers. This too would seem to me to be a mistake, as it may give a sense that the Bill of Rights is produced over the heads of most people and miss the opportunity to build consensus around it. As a Bill of Rights specifically for Northern Ireland, it is akin to a constitutional rights document, and most such documents around the world draw specifically on the experiences of the people for whom the constitution is designed. Those that are successful capture well the community's sense of what was wrong in the old order and the limits of agreement as to how the new should develop. International standards can certainly be a helpful guide as to how an emerging consensus over the terms of association in the new Northern Ireland should be concretely expressed, but must spring from rather than dictate to that consensus if it is not to prove fragile. Valuable though international standards have been in providing a basis for human rights critique at a time when establishing consensus seemed very difficult in Northern Ireland, it would be forgoing an important opportunity to cling too tightly to them when the chance for creating consensus now exists.

One must remember what a Bill of Rights is. It is a statement of broad principles or values that set the parameters of what society may decide to do collectively when such a decision impacts on the rights of individuals. The statements which endure, such as the US Constitution, are those which are sufficiently powerful to reflect widely held beliefs, but sufficiently broad to allow change to take place in terms of what specific laws or policies best represent those principles at any moment in time. Hence, rather than seeking to have a Bill of Rights provision prohibiting the eleven-plus selection exam (too narrow and lacking in guidance as to what school selection procedure might exist) it would be better to have something like a right of fair and equal access to education. One could then debate and through legislation examine which form of school selection procedure reflected this right. In drafting the Bill of Rights for Northern Ireland, the trick will be to identify those values or principles which have not adequately been reflected in Northern Ireland in the past, and on which there is consensus that guaranteeing them for all is essential to ensuring a just and democratic society. To the extent that such values are not adequately recognised in the ECHR, the Bill of Rights should seek to reflect them.

Before going on to discuss what those values might be, it is worth pausing to reflect on a crucial issue for the Bill of Rights, namely the extent to which it will have an impact beyond the State. This issue arises primarily because many would argue that the most significant human rights violations in Northern Ireland have been the responsibility not of the State but of armed opposition groups. As they correctly point out, over 90% of the killings and an even higher proportion of the injuries which have occurred in the Northern Ireland conflict can be attributed to groups such as the IRA, INLA, UVF and UFF rather than the police or army. What is less clear is the extent to which these involve human rights violations. Some human rights NGOs, such as Amnesty or Human Rights Watch, have taken up the issue of non-state actions, others have not. A common problem for both is what standard to apply. Human rights treaties generally only bind States, not private entities. Hence while the United Kingdom is under an international obligation not to torture anyone, none of its citizens individually have this obligation. An alternative is international humanitarian law, which binds all parties to a conflict. Going down this line involves both effectively granting equal recognition to the armed forces of all the parties to the conflict, something few critics of armed groups are willing to do, and accepting that each has a legitimate right to use even lethal force in some circumstances. While Amnesty has largely adopted this approach, it has struggled to identify exactly what violent actions of armed groups to condemn. 'Disappearing' or torturing people purely on the grounds of their community background is clearly beyond the pale, but what of killing the chief of police?

However, there is another way forward and one that it seems to me already finds some recognition in Northern Ireland. This is to fix the obligation on the State but to look at the totality of state action and how it can act effectively to protect the rights of all. The development of domestic violence in international human rights law is a good example of this strategy. Although violence against domestic partners is not generally conducted by the agents of the State, activists on the issue have pointed out that this does not free the State of all responsibility. There is an obligation to have laws on the books prohibiting such violence, for example not allowing partners a 'reasonable chastisement' defence, to ensure effective investigation and prosecution of such offences and to offer support to victims. Efforts to deal with corporate human rights violations by invoking the State's powers to issue or deny licences or credits is another example of how non-state abuses of power can be brought within the scope of state action. The extensive use of anti-discrimination law is one example of how we already recognise in Northern Ireland that protecting the human rights of all may require action by the State to regulate the conduct of private actors.

Ensuring the protection of the rights of all in Northern Ireland clearly requires more than curbing the power of an over-mighty State, important though this is. A range of private actors also wield significant power, the abuse of which can infringe the rights of others. The Bill of Rights should seek to address this in ways which are concrete and which go beyond simply condemning the actions of one group or another, valuable though this may be in the development of a community morality. The values which the Bill of Rights reflects should be values which all see as important for themselves, but also which they acknowledge they have an obligation to respect for others.

## Values and principles

So what are those values or principles which the Bill of Rights should seek to capture? I would suggest four: equality, accountability, freedom and democracy. A deficiency in each can be seen as centrally related to the problems of Northern Ireland, and in respect of each it is unclear to what extent the ECHR has provided adequate protection. The theme of inequality has long been seen by observers and participants as a central cause of conflict in Northern Ireland. Issues of inequality between Catholics and Protestants in housing and employment were at the forefront of early civil rights protests. Although significant legislative and institutional steps have been taken to rectify this, and significant progress has been made in a number of areas, the problem is far from being eradicated. Studies for the Patten Commission indicated that the police force remained less than 10% Catholic; recent monitoring figures have shown only about 25% Catholic representation in the senior civil service and, while no reliable figures have been published, it seems likely that the judiciary remains predominantly Protestant. Above all there remains the stubborn problem of Catholic male unemployment being over twice as high as that of Protestants, though it seems to be moving in the direction of greater equality since the Fair Employment Act, 1989. While such inequality persists, one section of the community may remain doubtful as to whether it is accepted as a full participant in society.

Turning to accountability, we can see that perceptions of a lack of accountability have been at the heart of many concerns regarding human rights in Northern Ireland. Such concerns have focused especially on the lack of accountability for the use of force, often lethal force, by both the state and armed opposition groups. Demands for the re-examination of Bloody Sunday, which have now borne fruit in the Saville Inquiry; for improved police complaints procedures, which have led to the establishment of a Police Ombudsman, and for information on the whereabouts of those 'disappeared' by paramilitary groups, which brought some response by the IRA, are all manifestations of this. Recurrent criticism of the inquest system in Northern Ireland, which in the absence of a prosecution is often the only form of judicial examination of killings by the army or police, also reflects a desire to ensure greater accountability. More generally it might be said that many in Northern Ireland have felt that the years of direct rule deprived them of any real form of accountability in respect of many decisions affecting their lives.

The related themes of freedom and democracy may seem somewhat trite in a human rights context. Surely the objective of all human rights instruments is to enhance freedom and democracy. Yet they are worth stressing precisely because the Northern Ireland experience has been marked by a significant lack of respect for freedom and democracy — notably the freedom of people to express their beliefs without fear, and for democracy as a way of resolving disputes through dialogue and compromise as opposed to the use of force. This can be seen both in respect of 'official' action such as the banning of Republican Clubs in the 1960s or the media restrictions of the 1980s and 1990s, and 'unofficial' actions such as campaigns of sectarian murder or intimidation. The annual summer conflict over disputed Orange parades most graphically captures the inability of some people to respect, or perhaps even comprehend, political views sharply opposed to their own.

A Bill of Rights could address each of these areas. In respect of accountability it could go beyond the limited provisions in Article 6 of the ECHR, on the right to a fair hearing in respect of private law rights, and Article 10, on the right to receive information, to establish stronger rights to freedom of information and fair administrative procedure. It could also provide clearer rights for victims of personal violence to obtain compensation or be kept informed of investigations. In respect of freedom and democracy it might strengthen the obligation on the State to prohibit harassment or intimidation on grounds of religion or political belief. It might also eventually strengthen the commitments currently contained in Section 30 of the Northern Ireland Act, to make political recognition and participation conditional on the severing of all links with private armies.

I will look in most detail at the issue of equality. How to achieve this remains a very difficult task in such a highly segregated society (in terms of housing, schools and cultural pursuits) as Northern Ireland. As Kevin Boyle and Tom Hadden have powerfully illustrated in their book, *Northern Ireland: The Choice*, two broad paths can be followed. One may be described as an integrationist approach, which would seek to ensure that everyone in Northern Ireland would have an equal opportunity to gain access to a range of shared goods, including jobs, government benefits or public offices. The other, which might be described as a separationist approach, looks to an equal division of goods between the two communities and then an allocation of the goods within that community. The first may be seen as more individualistic and orientated towards equality of opportunity, an example being the removal of barriers to equal opportunity in employment wrought by the Fair Employment legislation. The second is more communal in character and emphasizes equality of outcome, a prime example being efforts to ensure funding for Catholic maintained schools in Northern Ireland equal to that provided for (effectively Protestant) state schools. In trying to decide which model of equality might be pursued in Northern Ireland one can look to the Agreement for assistance.

At first glance it appears to incline to the separationist approach. The agreements for distributing ministerial office in the new Executive or for passing contentious legislation in the new Assembly, which require cross-community support, suggest society is to be structured on a division of spoils between unionist and nationalist. The stress on the composition of key institutions being 'representative of the community' (for example in legislation establishing the Human Rights, Equality and Parades Commissions, as well as in the reports of the Patten and Criminal Justice Reviews) and the need for 'parity of esteem' all incline to a conception of group rights and of equal shares for the two communities. Moreover neither the Agreement nor the Northern Ireland Act contains any commitment to seeking to reduce segregation, for example in housing or schooling.

However I would suggest there are other elements of the Agreement, broadly defined, which incline towards a different approach to equality. These include the fact that access to ministerial office remains tied to electoral success rather than purely to community affiliation, and that there remains the possibility that contentious legislation may be passed by a broad majority of the whole community, without achieving approval in both communities. Moreover Patten firmly rejected ideas of different regional police forces in Northern Ireland. These could, as in Belgium, have become the basis for different community police services, e.g. a 'Catholic' police west of the Bann and a 'Protestant' force east of it. While Patten's proposals recommend vigorous affirmative action measures in the sphere of police recruitment, these are envisaged as temporary in character, not a permanent feature of the police service. Furthermore, while the Northern Ireland Acts' *Section 75 equality duty* requires public authorities to assess whether their polices are having an adverse impact on one section of the community as opposed to another, the community in question is not limited to those defined by religion or political opinion, but is covered by a range of other criteria.

The Agreement therefore appears to preserve something of a tension between individualist, integrationist approaches to equality and their communal, separationist alternatives. In seeking to decide which should be reflected in the Bill of Rights, it appears to me useful to look to the relationship between equality and the other values I have suggested as lying at the heart of the conception of rights captured in the Agreement. I would suggest that the concept of accountability, and even more so those of freedom and democracy, incline us more in the direction of the first conception of equality: accountability, because in the end it stresses ideas of individual responsibility and rejects the idea that failure to reach certain standards may be excused if those of the 'other side' do likewise; freedom and democracy because they stress ideas of development and change through dialogue. They stand firmly against ideas of identity serving as destiny or of certain relationships being fixed forever. Moreover they acknowledge that people in Northern Ireland often have several identities and that while the division between Protestant and Catholic may be central it is not exhaustive.

Reflecting these different observations in a Bill of Rights provision is clearly no easy task, but I would suggest we are looking for something broad in character which seeks to ensure that a particular identity is not a hindrance to one's opportunities in life, nor a qualification for them. The Bill of Rights would thus contain provision for significant affirmative action measures designed to challenge the effect of past practices of discrimination, but would make clear that such are only permitted on a targeted and temporary basis. It would also provide for careful scrutiny of official policies to ensure that they do not reinforce patterns of disadvantage for particular groups. The provision contained in Article 14 of the ECHR, which is limited to prohibiting discrimination *in the enjoyment of other rights protected under the Convention,* is clearly inadequate for this task and a fresh provision will be required in this area. Recent constitutional provisions in other countries, such as South Africa or Canada, or other international human rights standards may provide more useful templates.

A Bill of Rights organised around acknowledging areas in which human rights protection has been deficient in Northern Ireland in the past, and which reflects on the extent to which the ECHR alone is unlikely to rectify this, should provide a sound legal foundation for the effective protection of human rights in the future. However, the world is littered with examples of impressive constitutional provisions which had little impact on the societies they were created for. If the human rights provisions of the ECHR and any Bill of Rights are actually to produce an improvement in the protection of human rights in Northern Ireland, there is also a need to examine the social and political conditions in which they will operate. The next section attempts to do this, and to identify where the potential resistance to such developments might come from.

## Challenges to the effective enforcement of Human Rights

New human rights laws in Northern Ireland will not enforce themselves. To be effective they will require that people are aware of them, that they have strong advocates, that a wide range of institutions respect them and that other institutions, notably the judicial and political institutions, enforce them if this is not the case. Above all there is a need for the development of a strong and broadly owned human rights culture in Northern Ireland. Without this, human rights may well remain marginal to the lives of many people.

### *Dealing with the Past: Should Northern Ireland have a Truth Commission?*

Since the late 1970s many societies emerging from a period of conflict, which usually featured significant acts of violence conducted with impunity, have instituted a Commission to examine what occurred in their past. Such institutions have varied significantly in their composition, resources and legal powers but all have included as a fundamental aspect the uncovering of the truth about serious allegations of torture or killings which have not been the subject of previous legal proceedings. Many of those involved in such Commissions have already travelled to Northern Ireland to share their insights into the value and problems of such processes. However, few have been able to offer a definitive view on whether these Commissions proved an unqualified benefit to the societies in which they were established, still less on whether such a Commission would be appropriate in the circumstances of Northern Ireland. The jury is still out on whether even internationally high-profile Commissions such as those in Argentina or South Africa actually produced truth or advanced reconciliation. To some, they have merely sustained old conflicts and inhibited the development of a new society. To others the limitations on the ability of the Commissions to bring perpetrators to justice, whether because of the existence of an amnesty provision, as in South Africa, or deliberate limitations on their scope, as in Argentina, have prevented them from fulfilling their function of re-establishing the rule of law and renouncing the culture of impunity. Their capacity to produce an objective truth remains disputed, still more the extent to which they have brought about national reconciliation.

Perhaps the least that can be said is that those countries that have instituted a Truth Commission as part of a transition agreement have not witnessed a return to the human rights violations which produced the call for its establishment. Such Commissions have played an important part in underpinning the development of a new culture of accountability for the use of power and of adherence to human rights values. In Latin America especially, the cycle of military coups which plagued the region for much of the twentieth century appears to have been broken, perhaps because the actions of the military were publicly documented, reducing the risk of collective amnesia which prevailed in the past. This would suggest that there is merit in the idea of a Truth Commission for Northern Ireland. Certainly there is much in the recent past of Northern Ireland on which the truth remains opaque. More than half of the deaths caused by army or police action have occurred in disputed circumstances which neither criminal prosecutions, when they have taken place, nor inquests have resolved. In many of the cases in which people have been killed at the hands of paramilitary organisations, no one has been brought before the courts. Allegations of collusion between the security forces and loyalist paramilitaries on the one hand or of involvement of senior republican politicians in terrorist activity on the other continue to rumble on in the background and further revelations regarding them have the potential to destabilise political progress. In a climate of political transition and of greater transparency due to the Human Rights Act and Freedom of Information Act it is likely that further revelations will emerge, especially as victims may seek to use such new legal instruments to explore what happened in their own cases. Moreover we are likely to witness continued political pressure for mini truth commissions on the Saville Inquiry model, to enquire into collusion allegations surrounding the murders of Pat Finucane or Rosemary Nelson, for example. More truth is therefore likely to emerge but in a partial, incomplete and contested way.

Rather than see allegations about the past continue to plague the future, it might be better to develop a process which allows for a comprehensive re-examination of the past and acknowledges the right of all victims to know the truth. While many problems present themselves on the organisation and scope of such a commission, plus the relationship between a Truth Commission and criminal prosecution, these are matters on which comparative experience can offer useful guidance.

However, deeper and more difficult political obstacles lie in the way and are likely to block the creation of any Northern Ireland Truth Commission in the immediate future. They lie primarily in the fragile state of the peace process itself. Truth Commissions have tended to occur in two situations. One, as in most of Latin America, is where those formerly in power have dramatically lost it and the new government has both the moral authority and the power to overcome any resistance or backlash the Commission might give rise to. The other, as in South Africa or El Salvador, is where the contending parties have clearly reached an agreement as to the way forward and have accepted that revelations about the past will not deflect them from that path. While Northern Ireland is more like the latter in that there is a negotiated settlement between the parties rather than a loss of power by the former rulers, we are still some way from saying that all those involved have given their unqualified commitment to implementing it. Moreover, some of the key players in this negotiated settlement have good reason to resist any thorough investigation into what their agents may have been doing during the years of conflict. These include the United Kingdom government, notably its military and security agencies, and the various paramilitary organisations such as the IRA, UVF or UDA. Revelations about the activities of the former might have ramifications which go well beyond Northern Ireland, while disclosures about the latter might undermine the credentials of political parties linked to them and perhaps even compromise the position of some key political actors. The Agreement lacked any commitment to establish or even explore the possibilities of a Truth Commission and no political party in Britain or Ireland has subsequently pushed the idea. It therefore seems highly unlikely that there will be any formal Truth Commission in Northern Ireland in the near future, and that instead the messy process of partial truth being revealed through specific judicial proceedings and investigative journalism will continue. History alone can tell whether this pragmatic process of selective examination of the past will prove to have been the best way towards an inclusive political accommodation. However, one consequence is that new structures to enhance accountability will be built on less secure foundations than they might have been.

*Failure to achieve a broad consensus of support for Human Rights*

Just as the Agreement was based on a broad consensus of support, so the United Kingdom government is likely to require a wide measure of support in Northern Ireland to enact any recommendations as to a Bill of Rights, especially if it contains provisions which cannot easily be tied exclusively to Northern Ireland. This means that those anxious to see a significant Bill of Rights enacted, and indeed to see human rights more effectively protected in general, need to ensure that the project has widespread political support. In effect this means ensuring that it has support in the unionist community. While unionists have often been the most enthusiastic advocates of a Bill of Rights in successive negotiations on the future of Northern Ireland, a substantial proportion of the unionist community may now have come to see human rights as essentially a nationalist issue, as was demonstrated in the response of some unionists to the appointment of the Human Rights Commission. They may feel that the further development of human rights laws and institutions, such as the Bill of Rights, offers them little. Opposing the reduction of human rights to a matter of sectarian trade-offs is clearly vitally important.

A number of strategies may be pursued to achieve this. One is to note that most of the human rights standards provisions applicable in Northern Ireland, notably the Human Rights Act, derive from international treaties to which the United Kingdom has committed itself. A second is to observe that these standards go well beyond the main issues of historical controversy in Northern Ireland to influence issues, such as the rights of women or children, which affect both communities. A third is to argue, as I have done above, that the development of a Bill of Rights for Northern Ireland must be based on a principled approach to the question of the extent to which current law fails to adequately protect the rights of all. Such an approach seeks to identify the extent to which everyone in Northern Ireland, unionists as well as nationalists, has been affected by denials of their human rights and to identify key areas in which change is necessary to prevent this recurring.

Developing a human rights culture will also require a constructive approach from nationalists, who historically have experienced more significant violations of rights by the State. As more people from a nationalist background assume positions of power in the new political climate, it is important that they too accept that power brings with it responsibility and that victims once are not victims forever. Nothing is more likely to engender cynicism with regard to human rights than the impression that some of its most enthusiastic advocates do not regard it as constraining them. Overall there is a need to build a culture where everyone recognises both that they are entitled to assert their own human rights but also that they have an obligation to respect and advance the rights of others.

## Threats of Renewed Violence

Greater respect for human rights will be easier to achieve in a climate of peace. Dealing with violence has been offered as a justification for practices that infringe human rights in Northern Ireland, as it has been in many other societies. Indeed there can be little doubt that law enforcement authorities are especially likely to ignore the rights of suspects when under pressure to prevent and punish serious crimes or when under threat to their own lives. It is hardly a matter of coincidence that allegations of ill-treatment in police custody, for example, have significantly declined in Northern Ireland since paramilitary cease-fires were declared. However, two groups in particular have the potential to increase the level of violence and hence produce renewed pressure to disregard human rights guarantees, namely dissident terrorists and those involved in drug-related crime. While failure to punish and seek to prevent such violence would itself constitute a breach of human rights, it is crucial that the means adopted do not themselves involve serious violations of rights. The response of two groups to any such threats will be vital, i.e. the police and the politicians.

In respect of the police, they must respond to any such threat through the implementation of laws and policies which are fully compliant with human rights standards. Significant recent reforms in the criminal law, notably the passing of the Regulation of Investigatory Powers Act, 2000, have been designed to ensure that the police have adequate powers to deal with serious criminal activity while remaining within the scope of human rights guarantees. One would hope that the police would not reach too easily for the rather more draconian powers contained in the Terrorism Act, 2000, some of which may not be consistent with the ECHR. More effective police oversight and complaints institutions, plus the potential of greater judicial scrutiny of their actions, should encourage the police to act in a way which respects the human rights of all. Yet most studies of policing suggest that such external checking measures may ultimately have less impact than internal police culture. Vigorous efforts will be required by senior police officers, and the Policing Board provided for under the Police Act, to ensure that this culture is one which evinces a knowledge of human rights standards and a commitment to their implementation.

Just as important may be the reaction of politicians. As always it may be tempting to seize on particular groups as the cause of all our ills and to advocate draconian methods to deal with them. Yet demonising specific groups has rarely been a constructive way to deal with societal problems and it is vital that politicians come to acknowledge that living in a society whose institutions respect human rights will mean that those institutions are at times constrained. More broadly it is crucially important that politicians, both in the Assembly and elsewhere, develop a constructive relationship with the new institutions designed to protect human rights, notably the Human Rights Commissions north and south of the border. Seeing these institutions as important elements of a fully democratic system, rather than mere irritants, as some politicians may be inclined to do, could play an important role in developing the sort of broad human rights culture discussed above.

## *Developing Adequate Mechanisms to Ensure the Enforcement of Human Rights*

If a broad human rights culture does develop, and if politicians and key institutions such as the police commit themselves to working within it, then concerns as to human rights violations may diminish considerably. It is unlikely that they will disappear entirely, and to this end it is important that there exist strong and effective mechanisms for ensuring the enforcement of human rights guarantees. The lack of such mechanisms in the past has clearly been a major contributor to the perception and indeed the reality of inadequate protection of human rights in Northern Ireland.

Perhaps the key institution with regard to enforcement of human rights guarantees is the courts. Experience elsewhere has indicated that a judiciary which approaches a Bill or Charter of Rights in a positive and imaginative way can make it come alive, can suggest the relevance of human rights guarantees to the lives of all those within the jurisdiction. The experience of the Supreme Court of

Canada in the years following the enactment of the Canadian
Charter of Rights in 1982 is a good example. Landmark decisions,
notably in respect of equality issues and the rights of native
Canadians, led to significant re-examination of government policies
and also gave rise to the growth of 'Charter Canadians', namely
groups who lacked political power but whose claims found some
recognition in the courts. On the other hand a narrow and restrictive
approach to human rights guarantees, which shows excessive
deference to government and minimises the impact of human rights
provisions on existing law, can quickly kill off interest in making use
of the courts to enforce human rights guarantees, even by those who
feel they have nowhere else to turn.

At the moment it is the current Northern Irish courts which will be
responsible for ruling on disputes relating to human rights
guarantees. Several commentators who have examined the record of
these judges over the past thirty years have expressed some reserva-
tions as to the possibility of these courts adopting a more positive
approach. The judiciary has worked in a difficult environment in this
time, not just because they have been terrorist targets themselves,
but also because emergency legislation passed by the UK Parliament
has directed them to make rulings which even some judges may feel
do not fully respect human rights. Despite this, the courts have
shown themselves to be independent of the executive and unwilling
to become rubber stamps for the latest policy designed to put those
seen as hostile to the State behind bars, notably in their ultimate
decisions to acquit those charged on supergrass evidence. However,
they have also displayed a very positivist and conservative approach

to the interpretation of statutes and a reluctance to entertain arguments based on international human rights standards. In areas such as emergency arrest powers, access to lawyers or the use of lethal force by the police or army, the approach of the Northern Irish courts has been essentially deferential to the State, with little sense of an alternative reality to the official line of the need for such measures to defeat terrorism. Some recent decisions in the field of judicial review, where people can seek a review of the lawfulness of administrative decisions, have suggested a move away from this, and indeed hinted at some members of the judiciary being willing to embrace new human rights provisions. However there is clearly a need for a significant change in judicial culture, of a rethinking of the relationship between citizens, the legislature, the executive and the courts, if this is to develop into an expansive approach to the interpretation of human rights law.

This may be assisted by changes in the composition of the judiciary. The Criminal Justice Review, while not examining the past record of the courts, did see a need for the judiciary to be 'reflective' of the Northern Ireland community. This would clearly require a significant increase in the number of women judges and perhaps in the number who are appointed from the nationalist community, though the Review surprisingly fell short of recommending the application of community background monitoring to the judiciary. Their preferred means of achieving this is through a more open and transparent appointments process, notably through the creation of a Judicial Appointments Commission which includes a number of people who are not judges or even lawyers, to replace the somewhat opaque arrangements which exist at present. However, such a Commission will take some time to produce significant change and may not produce that much change in any case, as the Criminal Justice Review recommends that judges continue to be drawn from the ranks of the legal profession, admittedly from a broader range within it.

Leaving aside the question of whether government will even implement these recommendations, some would see the need for a more radical measure, such as the creation of a new judicial institution to oversee the implementation of the Bill of Rights, as with the Constitutional Court in South Africa. This could draw its membership from a wider range of people, such as academic lawyers or even politicians, as with the US Supreme Court. It would have the merit of a fresh start and a focus purely on constitutional or human rights issues. Such a court might well be more likely to adopt an expansive approach to a Bill of Rights than judicial institutions of general jurisdiction, for whom human rights provisions are only one of the issues with which they deal. However it also risks rarefying human rights within the judicial structure and lessening the obligation on judges at all levels, including the lower levels where most people come into contact with the courts, to give effect to human rights standards. Moreover there appears to be little political will for such an idea, and significant judicial hostility. It therefore seems likely that the responsibility for giving effect to the new human rights laws will rest with the existing courts.

Courts are not the only agency that have an important role to pay as regards enforcement. Other public institutions like the Police

Board, the Police Ombudsman, the Parades Commission and the Equality Commission all have an important role to play in ensuring that a range of public institutions respect human rights, as broadly conceived. The most central of these institutions in the human rights field is the Northern Ireland Human Rights Commission. As we already have seen, it is the NIHRC which has the task of making recommendations on a Bill of Rights, reviewing potential legislation, conducting public education on human rights and advising government on what it needs to do to ensure compliance with human rights provisions. In addition it has powers to assist litigants who allege that their human rights have been infringed and to conduct investigations into 'such matters, as it considers necessary or expedient'. Both are new powers that were not available to SACHR and should enable the NIHRC to play a more active and effective role in securing the protection of human rights.

Whether the NIHRC does make a significant difference as regards the enforcement of human rights depends on two things, the resources it has and what it does with them. As regards the first, the Commission has most of the powers which the UN recommends for national institutions for the protection of human rights in its 'Paris Principles'. The one significant omission is the absence of powers to compel the production of documents and witnesses when conducting investigations. Since the Commission has only recently begun its first investigations, into parades and juvenile justice, it remains to be seen whether early government promises of co-operation are fully borne out and render this omission irrelevant. A larger concern for the Commission is the limited financial resources at its disposal, only £750,000 per year. Given that the legal budget of the old Fair Employment Commission alone exceeded £250,000 in its final year, one suspects that legal costs may consume a considerable proportion of this and leave a limited amount for other activity. This makes the issue of what the Commission does with its resources even more important. In its first year of existence the NIHRC produced an ambitious draft plan which committed it to initiatives over the next three years in nine areas including children's rights and the rights of ex-prisoners, of victims and of people discriminated against on grounds of their sexual orientation, in addition to the major project on the Bill of Rights. While such a broad range of objectives is laudable and has helped to counteract some initial controversy over the Commission's composition, when some unionists threatened but ultimately decided against legal challenge to its 'representativeness', it may stretch the Commission's resources too thinly. Given that resources are limited for legal challenges, the strategic use of cases will be especially important. To date the cases it has supported are mostly still pending, though it has intervened as 'friend of the court' in a number of high profile cases brought by other people. These include a challenge by two prospective QCs to the declaration they are required to make of being willing to act for the Queen, a challenge to the lack of women on the Parades Commission, and an effort to prevent the BBC's *Panorama* showing a programme on the Omagh bombing which the Commission felt might jeopardize a fair trial. All of the Commission's applications in these cases were unsuccessful but secured valuable publicity and visibility. In the longer term, it will be important for the Commission to be seen to be winning cases and establishing significant precedents if it is to be viewed as actually making a difference.

While the introduction of the NIHRC is a welcome move, and important official recognition of the need to ensure that protecting human rights goes beyond paper declarations, it would be unwise to rely on it entirely to enforce the new human rights guarantees. Indeed national human rights commissions around the word flourish best where they are situated in an environment of a strong and independent judiciary, lawyers willing and able to take up human rights cases and a vibrant human rights NGO sector. As indicated earlier in this paper, Northern Ireland has witnessed a significant revival in human rights NGO activity in the past decade and this has played an important role in the development of new human rights guarantees. It is important that this sector continue to flourish if such guarantees are to be effectively implemented, something that will require both continuing financial support for such groups and a broadening of their range of concerns beyond a primary focus on human rights issues related to the conflict.

## *The External Environment*

Human rights in Northern Ireland do not exist in a vacuum. We have already seen the extent to which developments in the rest of the United Kingdom, notably the introduction of the Human Rights Act, and at the European and global levels, have played an important part in the development of human rights guarantees in Northern Ireland. This influence is likely to continue. Northern Irish judges, in particular, are likely to look to how judges across the Irish Sea interpret the Human Rights Act, even if they also produce some local variations. Assembly members too will no doubt be influenced by developments in the Westminster parliament. Here the portents are not entirely encouraging. Having introduced the Human Rights Act, the Labour government has appeared to backtrack somewhat on its enthusiasm for a rights agenda. The potentially draconian Terrorism Act (which casts the net of anti-terrorist law much wider than the old PTA), caution on Freedom of Information legislation and the absence of any commitment to creating a human rights commission for England and Wales all appear to be moves in the opposite direction. Little now is heard of the commitment to put human rights at the heart of foreign policy.

The European level is a better environment for optimism. New directives passed in 2000 offer protection against race discrimination at a European level for the first time, and provide a more comprehensive framework for dealing with employment discrimination. This includes for the first time discrimination on the grounds of age and sexual orientation and will eventually require an extension of anti-discrimination legislation in Northern Ireland. Europe is gradually moving towards some sort of Charter of Rights for the European Union. While there are legitimate doubts as to whether this is necessary given that all EU states are already party to the ECHR, and while the UK government has indicated a reluctance to sign it where it goes beyond the ECHR, such a move does at least signal the increasing prominence of human rights in developments in European governance.

Another particularly important external influence is what happens with regard to human rights in the Republic of Ireland. This is of importance at both a practical and a symbolic level. On a practical level there is a good reason to have an equivalent human rights regime North and South to encourage the free movement of people between the different parts of the island. Especially when it comes to rights affecting people's personal lives, such as educational or religious rights, a lower level of protection may discourage people moving from the South to the North or vice versa. On a symbolic level, the Agreement's commitment to an 'equivalent' level of human rights measures in the Republic is clearly motivated not just by a concern to improve the situation south of the border but also to influence that north of it. Measures to improve human rights protections in the South, such as the introduction of a single Employment Equality Act in 1998, are likely to spark calls for improvement in the North, especially in light of developing contacts between the respective human rights and equality agencies. On the other hand more restrictive measures in the South, to deal with asylum seekers or to combat drugs for example, can only serve to weaken the position of those seeking to resist such measures in the North. The lessons of the curtailment of the right to silence in the South in 1984, which was subsequently invoked by those who did likewise in Northern Ireland in 1988, remain valid.

## Conclusions

Just ten years ago the prospects for human rights in Northern Ireland looked bleak. Emergency laws were still fully in force, the media ban and the curtailment of the right of silence had recently been introduced, the Stalker affair had come and gone without a clear answer on the existence of a 'shoot to kill' policy. However, as has been argued earlier in this paper, even at that time circumstances were changing for the better. These changes accelerated significantly with the onset of the peace process. Even if this process were to go into decline one may legitimately hope that the new human rights laws and institutions that have been created as a result of it would prevent a return to those bleak days of the 1980s.

However, even if the peace process and the new institutions of government do progress, an exponential growth of human rights cannot be taken for granted. Human rights may have moved from the margins to the mainstream but there remain doubts as to whether it has reached the heartlands. There is a clear need to deepen and broaden commitments to human rights: deepen such commitments so that some of those who may mouth commitments to human rights as the new orthodoxy actually begin to reflect on the implications it has for their own actions and come to take ownership of such issues; broaden such commitments so that a greater range of people come to see human rights as relevant to their own situation, but also to that of others. If the latter is not done there is a risk that while the human rights problems directly related to the unionist/nationalist conflict are reduced, those relating to groups such as children, women or ethnic minorities will only increase. Bold legal measures, such as a Truth Commission or an imaginative Bill of Rights, can make an important contribution to such a process. However, the task goes beyond simply the passing of new laws or the creation of new institutions. Rather it is to produce a culture in which people believe that respecting the rights of others will help to secure the rights they hold dear. If this is achieved, then Northern Ireland might well move from being a case study of human rights problems to providing a model of human rights achievement.

# Bibliographies

## A Human Rights Culture for Ireland? Ivana Bacik

Connelly, A., 'Ireland and the European Convention', in Dickson, B. (ed.), *Human Rights and the European Convention*. London: Sweet and Maxwell, 1997.

Constitution Review Group, *Report*. Dublin: Government Publications 1996.

Hogan, G., 'The Belfast Agreement and the Future Incorporation of the ECHR in the Republic of Ireland' 4 *Bar Review* 205-211, 1999.

Hogan, G. and Whyte, G., *The Irish Constitution: J.M. Kelly* (third ed.). Dublin: Butterworths, 1994.

Irish Commission for Justice and Peace, *Re-righting the Constitution: The Case for New Social and Economic Rights*. Dublin: ICJP 1998.

Klein, N., *No Logo*. London: Flamingo, 2000.

McColgan, A., *Women Under the Law*. London: Pearson, 2000.

McDermott, P., 'Evidence and Procedure Update' 3 *Irish Criminal Law Journal* 18-22, 2000.

Mullally, S., 'Equality guarantees in Irish constitutional law – the myth of constitutionalism and the "neutral" state', in Twomey, P. and Murphy, T. (eds.), *Ireland's Evolving Constitution 1937-1997*. Oxford: Hart Publishing, 1998.

Murphy, T., 'Economic Inequality and the Constitution' in Twomey, P. and Murphy, T. (eds.), *ibid* 1998.

O'Connell, D., 'The Irish Constitution and the ECHR: Belt and Braces or Blinkers?' *Irish Human Rights Review* 82-101, 2000.

Power, C., 'The Equal Status Bill 1999 – Equal to the Task?' 5 *Bar Review* 267, 2000.

Quinn, G., 'The Nature and Significance of Critical Legal Studies' *Irish Law Times* 282-290, 1989.

Whyte, G., 'The Application of the European Convention on Human Rights before the Irish Courts' 31 *International and Comparative Law Quarterly* 856, 1982.

## Human Rights and Northern Ireland: In from the Margins? Stephen Livingstone

Amnesty International, *Political Killings in Northern Ireland* (1994).

Committee on the Administration of Justice, *Civil Liberties in Northern Ireland* (third edition, 1997).

Dickson, Brice, 'Northern Ireland's Troubles and the Judges', in Hadfield (ed.) *Northern Ireland: Politics and the Constitution.* Open University, 1992, p. 130.

Hadden, Tom and Boyle, Kevin, *Northern Ireland: The Choice.* Penguin, 1994.

Hadfield, Brigid, 'The Protection of Civil Liberties in Northern Ireland' (1997) 3 *European Public Law* 513.

Harvey, Colin (ed), *Northern Ireland: Essays in Democratic Renewal.* Hart Press, 2001.

Harvey Colin, and Livingstone, Stephen, 'Human Rights and the Northern Ireland Peace Process' (1999) *European Human Rights Law Review* 162.

Human Rights Watch, *Human Rights in Northern Ireland* (1991).

Lawyers Committee on Human Rights, *At the Crossroads: Human Rights and the Northern Ireland Peace Process* (1997).

Livingstone, Stephen, 'The Northern Ireland Human Rights Commission' (1999) 22 *Fordham International Law Review* 1465.

McCrudden, Christopher, 'Mainstreaming Equality in the Governance of Northern Ireland' (1999) 22 *Fordham International Law Review* 1696.

Mageean, Paul and O'Brien, Martin, 'From the Margins to the Mainstream:
   Human Rights and the Good Friday Agreement' (1999) 22 *Fordham International Law Review* 1499.